NØT THE SAME GOD

Is the Qur'anic Allah the LORD God of the Bible?

Sam Solomon
with Atif Debs

Books and Other Publications by Sam Solomon

Sam Solomon, _A Proposed Charter of Muslim Understanding_, foreword by Gerard Batten, UK Independence Party, Member of the European Parliament for London.

Sam Solomon and E. Al Maqdisi, _The Mosque and It's Role In Society_

Sam Solomon, "The Challenge from Islam," Chapter 4 in the book: Ravi Zacharias (Author and General Editor), _Beyond Opinion: Living the Faith We Defend_

Sam Solomon and E. Al Maqdisi, _The Common Word: The Undermining of the Church_

Sam Solomon and E. Al Maqdisi, _The Modern Day Trojan Horse: Al-Hijra, The Islamic Doctrine of Immigration, Accepting Freedom or Imposing Islam?_

E. Al Maqdisi and Sam Solomon, _Al-Yahud: Eternal Islamic Enmity & the Jews_

Published by Advancing Native Missions
Charlottesville, Virginia, USA

NOT THE SAME GOD

Is the Qur'anic Allah the LORD God of the Bible?

Sam Solomon

with

Atif Debs

ANM
publishers

Advancing Native Missions
Charlottesville, Virginia, USA

Dedication

In this work, to the exclusion of the implications and consequences that flow from the core tenets of Islam as expounded in my previous books, I wish to shift the emphasis to that utmost tenet at the center, the foundational tenet that is the driver and binding force of them all—that of Islamic Monotheism, as encapsulated and expressed in the Doctrine of Allah, termed the Tawheed.

It has always been my desire to do my part, along with the growing numbers of other former Muslims, to shed light on the inevitable out-workings of what is veiled in the Qur'an—for the benefit of my Muslim friends to be able to break free, and for the Church to be better prepared to stand.

Vertically this book is dedicated first and foremost to the Triune LORD God of the Judeo-Christian scriptures, Father, Son, and Holy Spirit—the covenant making, the covenant keeping and the covenant sustaining God. The God who spoke to the Fathers in diverse manners, and in these last days has revealed Himself through His Son, for it is His joy to be known, and to reveal Himself. For He so loved the world that He gave His One and Only Son Jesus, that whosoever believes in Him, and in His substitutionary vicarious death on the cross of Calvary, His resurrection on the third day and His ascension to the right hand of the Father, according to the Scriptures, is saved, shall not perish but shall have eternal life.

Horizontally this work is dedicated to groups, and individuals:

The *first* group are those Christians who, through being forced to live either under the shadow or within the full reality of Muhammad's Dhimmitude laws whereby it is illegal to witness openly for their LORD, those who have experienced severe spiritual, societal, and even physical oppression, but have not given up.

The *second* group would be all those ex-Muslims who called upon Jesus and received His acknowledgment as their Lord and Savior, and through studying the Biblical scriptures, have stood their ground as well.

Thirdly, the Lord has placed many colleagues and yoke-mates within my life to enable my calling and ministry, and, in turn, for me to mentor. I dedicate it to them, as well.

I dedicate it to my courageous colleague Andrea Williams, and my precious sister, friend and intercessor Elizabeth Curry.

I also dedicate this book to my gracious, generous and bold friends: Tami & Andy Miller, Bjorn Larsen, Carrie Wesley, Gary & Linda, Kären, and Richard & Jane Elizabeth.

And *finally* this book is dedicated to my late colleague, friend and brother Elias Al-Maqdisi, who suffered much for his faith in Christ Jesus our Lord.

Sam Solomon

Acknowledgement

I want to thank all those who read this manuscript, commented, edited and proof read it for all their helpful comments.

I wish to thank all those who prayed—for without the blessings of the Lord—this book would not have been possible.

Sam Solomon

x

Table of Contents

List of Figures

List of Tables

Foreword by Colin Dye

The Qur'an claims that Allah and the God revealed in the Judaeo-Christian scriptures is one and the same being: "...our Allah and your Allah is one..." (Surah 29:46). That this is the correct interpretation of the Qur'anic teaching is without contention. However, Sam Solomon rejects this Qur'anic claim as utterly false and without foundation. Many will be shocked to hear this and, despite the carefully reasoned arguments he presents, will want to continue to assert that Islam is one of the "three great monotheistic religions" and that Jews, Muslims and Christians worship the same God. The reasons for the unwillingness to abandon this commonly-held position are serious and far-reaching. They demonstrate why Sam Solomon's significant and timely investigation into the Islamic doctrine of sameness is so necessary.

First, there is in the West an increasing impatience over religious debate. The growing secularisation of our Western societies means that religious arguments are increasingly regarded as distasteful. This is especially true when it comes to arguments between religions. The predominant viewpoint is that religious ideas are mere "faith" claims having no real connection with demonstrable truth or with reality as it exists. The inadequate yet increasingly accepted definition of faith as "believing without evidence" leads to the conviction that religious ideas are matters of only private or personal opinion and should never be admitted in the public arena for serious debate or used to build public policy.

However, this understanding of faith is highly unsatisfactory for Jews, Christians, and Muslims alike. All three religions make claims that can and should be the subject of objective enquiry. Christianity, for example, was birthed in the full blaze of history and the basic facts of the gospel story are verifiable through the accepted means of historical enquiry. Jesus was born in Bethlehem, conducted a messianic ministry in accordance with Hebrew prophetic predictions, claimed to be the Son of God and was executed during the time of Pontius Pilate and, after three days, was raised from the dead. Either these events happened as presented or they did not happen. Historical enquiry can settle the question.

Given this background it is easy to see how a book that challenges the truth claims of one religion against another will be viewed as breaking the rules, ignoring the rational and respectable Western approach to religious discussion.

By the same token, the Qur'anic claim that Allah is one and the same as the LORD God of the Bible must be submitted to objective enquiry. Sam Solomon argues that the Qur'an in its claim that Allah is the one God worshiped by all true Muslims, Jews and Christians is not valid. In fact, he demonstrates that Allah as presented in the Qur'an is so far removed from the God of the Bible as to be a totally different being without any commonality or sufficient similarity as to be reasonably presented as one and the same. In fact, Allah and the LORD God are so different that they cannot even be said logically to co-exist.

To insist that Jews, Christians and Muslims worship the same God because they all agree that there is only one God is to miss the point entirely. Either Allah is the one true God, or the LORD God is the one true God. One of them is an imposter, a non-existent being, an empty, idolatrous notion. A Hindu once argued that because he and I believe in a Supreme Being, that we both believe in the same God. The Christian and Hindu understanding of God is so different as to make any identification between the God and Father of Jesus Christ and the Hindu notion of a Supreme Being impossible. These two views of God are not only incompatible, but are also mutually exclusive.

By the same objective reasoning, there can be no confusing the God of the Bible with the Allah of Islam. The God of the Bible is transcendent and immanent, infinitely exalted above and beyond his creation, yet everywhere present in his creation. Allah is not. The God of the Bible is knowable. Allah is not. The God of the Bible seeks relationship with humanity, created in his image. There can be no relationship with the Allah of the Qur'an. The idea that humanity is made in the "image of God" is *shirk*. According to Islam, it is the unforgivable sin of idolatrously imputing partners, associates, or associations with Allah. The God of the Bible is the God of covenant relationship. Allah is so removed, above and beyond the created world, that he could never, under any circumstances, bind himself in covenant with anyone or anything.

The God of the Bible reveals himself in anthropomorphic and analogical language, in metaphors and similes by which he is compared to created things.

We learn the unlimited by means of the limited. Allah cannot be thus understood. He cannot be compared with anything, either within himself or outside himself, leaving us in ignorance of who he really is and what he is really like. He remains in all crucial respects unrevealed.

Most important of all, the God of the Bible makes himself known. He discloses himself through fellowship with Adam and Eve in the Garden, he meets with the Patriarchs, dwells in the Tent of Meeting in the wilderness and in the Temple of Jerusalem and, in the full and final revelation of himself, he comes down to earth in the Incarnation – God becoming man. He now lives in the hearts of believers by his Holy Spirit. All this is totally and undeniably impossible for the Allah of the Qur'an, who could never be confused with or identified as the God and Father of our Lord Jesus Christ. He is certainly not the one eternal Being who exists and always has existed in three divine Persons – Father, Son and Holy Spirit.

The second reason why this book is vitally important is that it exposes Islam to critical scrutiny. Ironically this is also why its conclusions will be unacceptable to many, both inside and outside Islam. Those living in or who have been raised in Muslim majority nations can be extremely intolerant of any criticism or questioning of Islam. In many of those nations it is religiously, culturally and even legally unacceptable to contradict Islamic teaching. But Muslims of every nation have a right to know at which points the truth claims of their religion are being sincerely questioned. They have a right to know that there are serious questions being honestly asked and honestly answered, even if the answers contradict what they have been taught. Religious ideas matter because truth matters and it is surely acceptable, even necessary, for religious people to examine their beliefs to see if they really are sustainable in the light of truth.

It is sad to see honest debate and critical analysis of Islam being stifled or prevented in the name of tolerance. A position is either valid or invalid and the only way to find out is to subject it to critical analysis. The desire is not to be deliberately offensive, but it is hard to see how a book that challenges Islamic teaching could avoid being critical. To do so, would not be in keeping with any sincere quest for truth. There is a world of difference between unfair and unnecessary attacks on Islam (or any other religion) and the spirit of free enquiry concerning all truth claims, even Islamic ones. How could a believer in the Bible fail to compare Islamic teaching concerning Allah with the God revealed in the Biblical record? And having done so, how can this same believer be reasonably expected not to contradict the false claims of the Qur'an whenever they are exposed?

Either the Islamic claim is correct or it is not. If the Qur'an is wrong in what it says about sameness then the error is not an inconsequential one. To accept it as true is to accept it together with all its ramifications. One is also obliged to accept the Islamic explanation as to why the Biblical scriptures differ so vastly from the Qur'anic account. The Qur'an teaches that the Judaeo-Christian scriptures have been corrupted. The prophets were all Muslims, slaves of Allah, whose main role was to point towards the Messenger to come, Muhammad, who was to be the "seal of the prophets". The Bible, as we have it today, is then characterized as being totally unreliable and defunct as a book of truth and revelation. There is no historical, critical or documentary evidence to support this Islamic version of events. Therefore, to accept the Islamic teaching on sameness is simply and blindly to submit oneself to the Qur'an. The stakes are as high as that.

Notwithstanding this reality, many Christian missionaries and apologists deny that the Qur'an teaches the Bible has been corrupted. They cite the Qur'an as saying Islam's prophet was instructed to learn from the "people of the book". But Sam Solomon shows that this is a mishandling of the Qur'an as every true Qur'anic interpreter knows. We can bury our head in the sand no longer. We must abandon any doctrine of sameness – if for no other reason than to begin to approach our Muslim friends and colleagues with the correct understanding of what Islam teaches, and not what we think it teaches. This must apply to all our communication with Muslims. To base Muslim-Christian relations, dialogue or even evangelism on a false notion of sameness leads to confusion at best. To be truly tolerant, every aspect of Muslim-Christian communication and relationship must be based on a correct understanding of one another's claims and religious positions.

The final reason I put forward as to why this book is so important and why its message must be heeded has to do with cultural understanding and the importance of Muslim-Christian and Muslim-Jewish relations. The antipathy shown towards Muslims in Western nations based on misunderstanding and misrepresentation of Islam and motivated by racial prejudices or cultural stereo-types is often called "Islamophobia". Surely by the same token we cannot build tolerance and community cohesion based on misunderstandings and misrepresentations of one another's religions. It is the contention of this book that Islam grossly misrepresents Jewish and Christian teaching on the nature of the God of the Bible by identifying him with the Allah of the Qur'an. It also argues that we grossly misrepresent Islam if we agree with its teaching on sameness while denying its claim that the Bible has been changed and corrupted and that the prophets were all Muslims proclaiming the Islamic oneness of Allah, and calling for faith in his messenger.

This is not an irrelevant argument between people of different world faiths. What is at stake here is not the minutiae of hair-splitting distinctions which in the end are of no practical significance. All ideas have consequences and the Islamic teaching on sameness, if it continues to go unchallenged, will have vast geopolitical consequences. Strict sameness doctrine forces an Islamic interpretation on Judaism and Christianity and leaves no place for dissenting voices. Tolerance for any other religious view other than Islam is precluded. All cultures other than the Islamic culture are then unacceptable. Ultimately, no other society other than an Islamic society will be permitted.

In this book Sam Solomon and Atif Debs draw on Qur'anic scholarship to present a clear and compelling case to reject this false identification of Allah with the God of the Bible. The LORD God of the Bible looks for loving relationship with the people he created and longs to reveal himself to whomever wills to hear him and know him. He draws close and invites people of all nations humbly to come to him and meet him. This is the one, true and living God.

Colin Dye
December 2015

Colin Dye – is Senior Minister of Kensington Temple and leader of London City Church, a vibrant and dynamic multi-ethnic church organized into cells that are active across London. He has authored over 40 books and is keen to see the church engage in today's society in ways that are both relevant and powerful.

Introduction

Statement of the Problem

Before we can analyze, we need to get the premise of the problem clearly in our minds, as well as those factors that block the elucidation and articulation of the true reality behind the phenomenon that is Islam.

The overall problem we have in even approaching the subject is that Islam is a multi-dimensional and dynamic reality and historic force, which sometimes sleeps, other times leaps, and always remains relentlessly patient—with unswerving confidence in the prevailing sweep of history and its own claimed "truth" and inevitability.

When Muhammad came on the scene in 610 AD, we are informed from Islamic sources that he explicitly proclaimed first and foremost, that he was the final "expected one," the prophet of Allah, as he said had been predicted in the Judeo-Christian scriptures—thus, from the outset establishing the grounds for the charge of Biblical corruption, although this would not be proclaimed fully as an official doctrine till many years later.

Subsequent to this initial proclamation of prophethood, he would then very quickly "receive inspirations" via an angelic being to proclaim that in his role as the expected one, his "mission" would not be to bring anything "new" but rather it was to "warn" and "correct"—to "warn" all around him, pagans, Christians and Jews, of the impending doom if they did not "go back" to the original "monotheism" as expressed in the belief in the one true god, Allah.

As time went on he would "correct" the existing Biblical narrative by incorporating the basic Biblical timeline but infusing it with Islamized events, rituals, and personalities (termed prophets and/or messengers) starting with Adam and proceeding through many of the Biblical characters including Ibrahim, Musa, Dawood and Issa, and ending with himself as the expected one, "the seal of the prophets".

In summation, the clear implication from the outset of Muhammad's self-claimed prophetic "call", is that the Qur'an would claim the "corruption" of the Biblical narrative, as the Bible does not have any references to Muhammad.

Implications of the Problem

Due to presumed apparent similarities there are various assertions by respected Christian (and Jewish) scholars who would posit that Jews, Christians, and Muslims believe basically in the "same" god. Some modern Christians would go further to develop "methodologies" for dialoging and reaching Muslims on the basis of this "sameness" or what some would term "sufficient similarity."

But this assumption of some level of similarity does not benefit anyone, as it is not based on the truth of the matter. Rather it obscures the stark differences between the Allah of the Qur'an and the LORD God of the Bible, as well as the bold claims of Muhammad as having been the fulfillment of the Biblical scriptures—thus resulting in the confusion of the issues for all: Christians and Muslims alike.

Our Position

So to put it simply, the "problem" at hand is to define and then explain and defend this position—that notwithstanding many apparent similarities, the Allah of Islam as expressed in the Doctrine of Islamic Monotheism (i.e. Tawheed) is the diametric opposite of the Triune LORD God of the Bible: Opposite in nature, character, knowability, description, and attributes. To do so would require an objective assessment based on the authoritative Islamic sources as well as the very words and expressions of the Biblical scriptures.

Keep in mind that the Islamic sources (The Qur'an and Sunnah) are integrated and intertwined. As a result, Muhammad's actions, pronouncements, and explanations have also become authoritative, known as the Sunnah.

The Qur'an, although seemingly innocent—its main objective was and is to undo the message and mission of Christ. We shall demonstrate in the following pages the various means that the Qur'an deployed to achieve its principal objective.

The Qur'an attempts to achieve this objective through a process of recasting of the Biblical events, personalities, rituals, and doctrines, all of which point to Christ—known in Christianity as the "Crimson Thread". The Qur'an accomplishes the total removal of this Biblical thread by revising and redirecting it to establish an alternative Qur'anic thread, or in Islamic terms, a pathway, that points instead to Muhammad as the "seal of the prophets", all the while keeping the illusion of being the fulfillment of the Biblical scriptures.

What this Book is NOT about, and WHY?

It is NOT about promoting a "methodology" on the part of a growing number of evangelical Christians to "engage" and ultimately reach Muslims, although it will—most definitely—greatly impact how a Muslim is approached with the truth of the Biblical "gospel".

NEITHER is it merely about what Muslims "do" individually or corporately (such as the spectrum from the "Moderates" to the "Jihadists") in response to their level of understanding of core Islamic texts, although—once more—it will provide the foundational perspective and tools needed to make that call.

So, this treatise is NOT about the details, rationales, and mechanisms of the key issues to be itemized below, issues which were not hidden in the dark, but began emerging, some out in the open, others less detected until recent years—during the three and a half decades since the 1979 establishment of the first modern Islamic State by the Ayatollah Khomeini in Iran. These specific emanations, though alarming, are the out-workings (call it the "fruit) of the core theological component of Islam (i.e. the Tawheed).

Given that Islam is not just a religion, but is an all encompassing socio-religious, socio-political, socio-economic, educational, legislative, judiciary, and militaristic system, cloaked and garbed in religious terminology—the composite global challenge of the Islamic system to the church and the world can be broken down into four categories, or separate but intimately interconnected "challenges": The Theological Challenge, the Political Challenge, the Administrative Challenge, and the Pragmatic Challenge.

The foregoing four challenges are put forth and delineated by this author in the book, "*Beyond Opinion: Living the Faith We Defend*", edited by Ravi Zacharias, Chapter 4 entitled, "The Challenge From Islam" [Ref. 1].

But this current book will focus primarily but not exclusively on the theological challenge, as the other three challenges all emanate directly from the first to accomplish the completed Islamic mandate. This separation is necessary, so that we can first grasp the reality of what the Qur'an says about Allah, his "creation", and what he expects of Muslims and mankind.

To that end:

- It is NOT about the establishment and furtherance of the ISIS "Caliphate" in Iraq and Syria—with an eye to the greater "Levant".

- It is NOT about the consequent demise of the Christian presence under the rule of ISIS, and other Islamists groups—through beheadings, slavery, and the application of "Dhimmi laws".

- It is NOT about the global "immigration" of Muslims coming to the West along with the fleeing Christian populations of Middle Eastern countries.

- It is NOT about the wide-ranging so-called "lone wolf" acts of terrorism/jihadism attributed to the so-called "fanatics" or "Islamists".

- It is NOT about the self-segregation that exists and is being perpetuated within Muslim communities in host countries in Europe, the U.S. and other parts of the non-Muslim world.

- It is NOT about the mechanism of the "Islamization" process, which is being implemented by immigrant Muslim communities within host countries (such as changes in school curricula, Islamic finance, dietary laws, etc.)

- It is NOT about the charges of "Islamophobia" being attributed to any criticism of Muslims or Islam.

- NOR is it about those seemingly "hopeful" attempts by "moderate" Muslims to "deny" the "harsher" tenets of Islam, and to present a "hopeful" face of "reform".

Keep in mind that the word "Islam" means, "surrender", and the word "Muslim" is a Qur'anically coined word meaning "surrendered to Allah". Therefore a Muslim's actions and beliefs, i.e., what he will think and "do" in a given circumstance—will of a necessity reflect what "Allah says" in the Qur'an, as interpreted in the Sunnah and by the scholars.

A major complicating factor, however, is that in advocating actions like those listed above, the Qur'an itself also makes the foundational claim that Allah is precisely the "same" deity as the LORD God of the Judeo-Christian scriptures, so thus becomes the final and best reason for the main question of the book, "Is the Qur'anic claim that Allah is one and the same as the LORD God of the Bible valid?"

How This Book Is Organized

The main theme of this book is that it should be clear to any objective observer that the Allah of Islam has no resemblance whatsoever to the LORD God of the Bible. Yet many Christian scholars and theologians have bought into the idea that there is such a resemblance. They used those Biblical characters who appear in some form in the Qur'an to establish so-called, "bridges of understanding" in order to dialogue and engage with Muslims and to bring them to the knowledge of the full Triune LORD God of the Bible.

In the pages to follow we demonstrate that this is a hopeless quest, not only because it has no basis in objective analysis of the respective scriptures, but even more importantly, because it falls into an Islamic trap! We make our argument in three steps in chapters 2, 4 and 6. Chapters 3 and 5 provide needed background information. Chapter 7 at the end provides a summary and a conclusion.

In *Chapter 1* we introduce the theme of this book whether the Allah of Islam is one and the same as the LORD God of the Biblical scriptures. One may be surprised to discover that the main reason this issue is even considered is due to the Islamic assertion of "sameness" or "theological equivalence" between the two. Not only that we demonstrate that this "sameness" permeates the Qur'an and Islamic doctrines to establish that the Islamic claims that the truth lies in what is termed "Islamic Monotheism" (Tawheed). This would introduce the reader to what we call the "Theological challenge" of Islam, to posit it as the driver of three other challenges: Political, administrative and pragmatic. The collection of these challenges would arise because Islam in reality is not a "faith" in the Western sense, but an all encompassing "system" or ideology, driven by a theological assertion that is aimed at countering the message and mission of Jesus Christ.

As we try to unfold this situation we are reminded that the Biblical narrative is based on a totally different theology—a theology based on the relationship between the LORD God and man, whom He created in His own image. As a result, the Bible deals with a covenant making and a covenant fulfilling God—with the fulfillment carried out at Calvary. We discover that "all scripture" speaks of Christ through foreshadowings and typologies—all spoken by the Lord Himself. This would pose the central corollary question: How do we know our God? Is it because He wants us to know Him intimately and positively? Or is it by leaving signs of his existence and relating to us via commands and directives? In attempting to discover the answers, we realize that we have entered into a divergent path, with no hope or the possibility of any commonality. But this would require careful examination and study of the primary sources of Islam (Qur'an and Sunnah/ Hadith) and the Bible itself.

In *Chapter 2* we substantiate the argument that the "sameness" of the Allah of Islam and LORD God of the Bible is rooted in the Qur'an itself. The Qur'an declares clearly that there is only one god, Allah, and that this god is the same as the one who "sent" the various prophets and messengers culminating in the final messenger, Muhammad.

According to the Qur'an, the Tawrat, Zaboor, and the Injeel (said to be the Torah, Psalms and the Gospels) all spoke of Allah, the same Allah that Muhammad proclaimed. This Islamic claim is then confirmed by the method in which the Qur'an and all previous divine books "came down"— basically from the same source, i.e. the "Eternal Tablet". It follows that if they all came from the Eternal Tablet, then clearly they all would have had the same original narrative. But of course, the completion of the record would arrive with the final version of the Qur'an as "brought down" to Muhammad by a complex process called "Wahy," the details of which are provided in Chapter 3.

But if this were true, what is to be done with the Biblical scriptures that existed long before Islam?

The only Islamic answer is that these Judeo-Christian scriptures conflict with the Qur'an because they have been corrupted.

There is confusion on this issue as well, as some Christian scholars argue that the Qur'an did not make a claim of Biblical corruption. Therefore, we go into detailed analysis to show how deep in the primary sources of Islam (i.e. Qur'an and Sunnah/Hadith) is this clear and unequivocal claim of Biblical corruption.

Before getting deeper into the issues of both the Islamic counter narrative and the resultant Biblical corruption claim, we provide in *Chapter 3* an important piece of the puzzle on "how" the Qur'an was "revealed" and the Sunnah was "formed". We describe that the processes involved are shrouded in secrecy, especially since, as we will see later in Chapter 6, Allah neither reveals himself nor does he communicate directly with his human slaves, even when they are his so-called messengers. The process of bringing down revelations has four important components, all of which are encapsulated in the doctrine of "Wahy", that is, Islamic inspiration.

In *Chapter 4* we illustrate our arguments further in relation to the stark divergence of the Qur'an/Hadith from the Biblical scriptures into the construction of a narrative that counters the "Crimson Thread" narrative of the Biblical scriptures. Here we delve into the analysis of those presumably "similar" characters as they appear in the pages of the Qur'an.

We limit ourselves to just a few: Adam, Noah, Abraham, Moses and Jesus. In reality a full study of all these supposedly "similar" characters is urgently needed, but for the purposes of this book, we limit ourselves to these five.

What is gained from this comparison is that, through a process of denials, omissions, replacements and additions, the Qur'an has created different versions of the Biblical characters, with similar sounding names, but with stark differences in the nature of their missions, storyline details, outcomes—in short a completely new and different narrative.

Chapter 5 then goes into the central question: "Who is this Allah?", which leads to the following further questions: What did he create? How did Muslim scholars through the centuries develop the "Tawheed" characterization? If Allah is basically the same as the LORD God of the Bible, then why is he limited, yet absolutely powerful? Why belief in Allah alone is not sufficient? Why is it *forbidden* to ask any questions about the *nature* of Allah? And we conclude as well with the issue of the "Love of Allah".

But in the final analysis we discover that it is the finality and indispensability of Muhammad that would drive the Islamic theme.

As the reader needs a historical perspective on how all of that developed originally, we focus on a historical flashback as given in *Chapter 6*. The reader is left to judge how Muhammad built the case for Islam as a carefully constructed process—a process that evolved as reactions to his initial proclamations of Tawheed and the Shahadah were first done privately to gain traction and inner circle credibility. But when he came out publicly with his open call (Da'wa) to go "back" to "Islamic monotheism", he managed to play the "People of the Book" card very effectively. In the end, Muslims were under the obligation to Islamize the world through the message of the Shahadah/Tawheed.

The concluding *Chapter 7* would recap the developments in the first six chapters to fully cement the conclusion, that the ideology of Islam and the theology of Biblical Christianity are mutually exclusive. This incongruity may disappoint some people who have built hopes not only on commonality and "sufficient similarity", but even on the two being the "same." However, the primary sources support our conclusion. So where is the hope for Muslims?

The "hope" of course is in the God who loves, cares, reveals Himself, and commits.

Style, Translations, Use of Symbols and Terms

In order to facilitate the use of supporting references and other materials we have resorted to explanatory footnotes. The reader may discover some necessary repetitions in the footnotes. This is because of the abundance of unfamiliar Arabic terminologies.

All the emphasis points, such as the use of *italics*, **bold** fonts, underlines, and explanatory brackets ( ) or [ ], are used to provide clarity.

The Biblical quotations are all from New International Version (NIV) Bible translation.

The Qur'anic quotations are based mainly on the author's translations from the Arabic original, while consulting a variety of online translations by Yusuf Ali, Al-Hilali, Sahih International, Pikthall, Royal Aal Albayt Institute, and possibly others.

The book uses two important terms consistently: LORD God and Allah.

According to the Bible the LORD God (Yahweh in Hebrew) is the covenantal revealed name of the triune God, with a meaning that has profound theological implications in Christianity. The use of this name for the God of the Bible is done throughout the book.

According to Islam and the Qur'an, Allah is the name given to the one deity that was already known to the pagan Arabs as the supreme being. It is beyond the scope of this book to address the issue of Arab Christians' usage of the term "Allah" when referring to God. Hence, "Allah" in this book refers only to the supreme deity of Islam.

The appendices provide supporting materials on the Islamic term "Tawheed", and also include an important "fatwa" (Islamic edict), on the "love of Allah."

The bibliography is selective and focused on the themes of the book.

Chapter 1

Lord God vs. Allah: The Sameness Illusion

Setting the Stage

In the Gospel of John, the Lord Jesus Christ declares, "*Then you will know the truth, and the truth will set you free.*" (John 8:32). In the same Gospel, Jesus would reply to his questioner, " *... I am the way and the truth and the life. No one comes to the Father except through me.*" (John 14:6). Thus in the final analysis, "truth" is embodied in the person of Christ Himself, as encapsulated in John 1:1, "*In the beginning was the Word, and the Word was with God, and the Word was God.*"

What a brutal blasphemy, a Muslim scholar would declare. After all, according to Islam, the full and final "truth" is in the Qur'an, which is authored by Allah himself, completed and kept unchanged in the original Arabic language. Allah would declare in the pages of the Qur'an, "*... There is nothing like Him (i.e. Allah)...*" (Surah 42:11).

And Muslim scholars, regardless of denominations and affiliations, would interpret this verse (Ayah) as a complete rejection of any "likeness", "image", "partner", "associate", or any form of direct revelation, and certainly not the "incarnation" of the creator of the heavens and earth. Allah is seen to be above all these considerations, in another world, beyond any possibility of being known. The only thing we can know is his "will" that he chose to reveal to selected "messengers" via intermediary angelic beings.

Philosophically, the Islamic Doctrine of Allah (termed the Tawheed) fits closely to the definition of "via negativa", as defined in Oxford Dictionary, it is: "A philosophical approach to theology which asserts that no finite concepts or attributes can be adequately used of God, but only negative terms."[1]

Yet some of the most outspoken "Christian" theologians/scholars would without hesitation, declare that, "Muslims and Christians believe in the same God," based on "sufficient similarities", as has Professor Miroslav Volf in his

---

[1] http://www.oxforddictionaries.com/definition/english/via-negativa

many books, culminating in "*Allah—A Christian Response*". Even prior to that, Volf was the prime mover in authoring and furthering the official Christian response to the "Come to a Common Word Between Us and You" interfaith initiative put forth by 138 Muslim scholars in the autumn of 2007, based on the key premise that the main "commonality" between Islam and Christianity is the "love of God and love of neighbor". Some 300 Christian theologians would initially accept this Muslim "invitation" (as it was termed), although some 20 have since officially removed their names.

This brings us to ask the main question, "Is the Qur'anic claim that Allah is one and the same as the LORD God of the Bible valid?"

Many who would yearn to find a better means of "engagement", or some form of "peace" or accommodation, would state that the "differences" one observes between the Biblical and the Qur'anic versions of the nature of the "creator of the heavens and earth" are best explained by a communication impasse, or a misunderstanding, based perhaps on "insufficient" information. Further, some Christian scholars would even venture to state that if Muhammad had full access to the Biblical scriptures, he would not have had such an incomplete and flawed understanding of the God of the universe. Even so, they say, what Muhammad provided, though incomplete, was a major step in the right direction. This rather charitable assessment did not take into account the gravity of the fact that he was claiming divine inspiration for this apparent "misunderstanding".

And then comes an increasing number of missiologists who would like to find some "common ground" or a "bridge" as in the Common Word exchange described above, to pave the way for Muslims to see the full reality of the Christian message. Their perspective is, simply why focus on the "differences", which they insist would predictably lead to divisiveness, rejection and animosity? Instead, they say one must start with the "similarities" and use those to establish a bridge to the fuller knowledge of the true God.

Therefore, in order to answer the main question of this book, we are necessarily sidetracked to deal with these apparently ancillary, but important, issues of alleged compatibility that have arisen among some Christians.

In reality, far from being "ancillary", we will demonstrate from the Qur'an and other Islamic sources that these apparent "similarities"—interpreted by many as "commonalities" or "bridges"—are nothing but direct and indirect claims made in the Qur'an and elsewhere by Muhammad himself, for the purpose of establishing credibility among the pagans of Mecca, and spiritual authority for his ultimate claim to the Jews and the Christians of his day of being the fulfillment of the prophecies of their scriptures.

Further, we will demonstrate that far from being "misunderstandings", these "differences" form a recognizable and intentional pattern that can easily be traced throughout the Qur'an, and the purposes for these changes identified.

The "Sameness" Illusion Defined

Islam is portrayed by many secular and Christian scholars as one of the three great Abrahamic monotheistic religions, and Allah as just another name for the same God—although escalating events throughout the world during the past three and a half decades or so have led increasing numbers of people to question if the Allah of Islam is indeed one and the same as the LORD God of the Judeo-Christian scriptures.

The Qur'an itself claims this sameness in unequivocal terms throughout—but explicitly in the following Surah, and in many other supporting references laying claim to further similarities:

> "...*Our Allah and your Allah is one...*" (Surah 29:46)

This direct claim, and apparent self-identification by Islam with the Judeo-Christian concept of "Monotheism" and previous revelations explains "why" so many Christian scholars have been so excessively drawn to these and other Qur'anic claims of "sameness"—similarities which at first glance give the strong appearance of agreement with much that is in the Bible—but which melt away when brought under scrutiny in comparison with their doctrinal or historical counterparts.

By definition, even cleverly designed "similarities" stop short of true "sameness", as clearly demonstrated in the extreme physical "similarity" of a counterfeit bill[2] and its original. A masterfully designed counterfeit bill may

---

2 Meaning a "currency note".

look precisely identical, and it even may get past any number of exchanges before it gets detected as fraudulent. But no one would be so foolish as to say, or even to think, "Well, it's almost perfect, so what difference does it make?" No one would be foolishly bold as to make the argument of "sufficient similarity" in regard to currency. Yet in the realm of the spiritual, such clear and rational standards are relaxed in the name of "tolerance for diversity" under the broad umbrella of considerations for "cultural context", or in regard to the variously expressed "fears", including, the "fear of offending" and the "fear of being unloving". So in this matter before us, we find that it is no longer an issue of discernment of "truth" to live by, to stand for and to defend, but is rather an issue of reconciling or coming to terms with differences.

The desire to engage with Muslims must not render one insensitive to the realities of Islam, so that to explain away foundational "differences" in the Qur'an, such as the nature of God Himself as an "incomplete" but "sincere" misunderstanding on the part of Muhammad defies both logic and the Biblical definitions of revelation and prophethood. Yet there is the tendency to extend Biblical definitions to be able to accept some form of truth or validity of Muhammad's account in the Qur'an.

To briefly demonstrate the extremes that are based on the above sufficient similarity measure, many will go on to propose that, since the Qur'an came seven centuries after Jesus Christ, but includes versions of the Biblical prophets and Jesus, the Qur'anic account itself then serves as a witness "pointing back" in time to validate Jesus in some imperfect, but partially valid form. This is in disregard of the fact that Issa (the Jesus of the Qur'an) did not die, was not resurrected, and came solely for the purpose of foretelling that the "expected one" to fulfill the scriptural prophesies would be "Ahmad", another of the names of Muhammad. Even so, some others in this camp go even further to posit that a Muslim who comes to be a "follower of Jesus" must NOT leave Islam, but must retain his legal and cultural identity as a "Muslim", and should then "follow Jesus" by continuing to worship in the Mosque, while praying secretly to Jesus, and being "salt and light" within the Islamic "Ummah", or community.

The Pivotal Question

Therefore, the *pivotal* question before us is, "Is the Allah of Islam <u>really</u> one and the same as the LORD God of the Bible?"

Is he the Triune God, the Creator God who made man in His own image—then walked, talked and fellowshipped with Adam, and later spoke directly to Abraham, Isaac, Jacob, Moses, and a long line of prophets? Is Allah the covenant making, the covenant keeping, the covenant sustaining God who willingly revealed Himself to mankind, and reaffirmed His presence and plan through succeeding generations of characters and events in Biblical history? Is he then the incarnational deity referred to by Isaiah as being, *"Emmanuel, God with us..."*(Is. 7:14)?

Indeed, is he the same deity who spoke through Jeremiah, asserting rhetorically,

> *"Am I a God at hand, says the Lord, and not a God afar off?"* (Jer. 23:23)

And finally, is he the God who was fully revealed in the person, life, death, and resurrection of Christ Jesus?

In short, is Allah the same deity as successively revealed within history throughout the entire Biblical text as the Alpha and the Omega?[3] Or, is he quite different, in both nature and purpose?

To answer these questions, we must focus exclusively on the theological challenge of Islam—as expressed in the central doctrine of Islamic Monotheism called "Tawheed", meaning the "absolute oneness", "unity" or "purity" of Allah. We should keep in mind that since Islam is a system covering every aspect of life, not just a religion, there are three other challenges tied to it which provide the various "out-workings" of this theological base, including the means of implementation, governance, spread, and consolidation, which I have delineated and explained in another work

---

[3] See for example *"He (Jesus) was chosen before the creation of the world, but was revealed in these last times for your sake"* (1 Peter 1:20), the *"Alpha and the Omega"* (Rev. 1:8a & 22:13), and *"All inhabitants of the earth will worship the beast—all whose names have not been written in the Lamb's book of life, the Lamb who was slain from the creation of the world."* (Rev. 13:8)

to include the Political Challenge, the Administrative Challenge, and the Pragmatic Challenge.[4]

Briefly, the Political Challenge is that Islam is at the same time a "religion and a state". The Administrative Challenge refers to the issues of implementing and maintaining Shariah law and its various branches. But the Pragmatic Challenge is more complex, and controversial, as it has to do with the means provided through Muhammad's Sunnah of handling objections to its advancement and acceptance among its adherents as well as among non-Muslims.

However, it is the theological aspect, and in particular the doctrine of the Tawheed which is the driver, as the others are simply out-workings of this theological foundation. But we have a problem here in regard as to how we must refer to the "theological" factor.

Biblical Theology and the Unknowability of Allah

This brings us to the key consideration of the full Islamic objections to the mean-ing, in fact the very idea of "Theology"—the study of the nature of God.

This instantly becomes problematic, Islamically speaking, since Allah is "unknowable" except for his revealed "will"[5], so the term "Theology" is not applicable within Islamic scholarship, but would be considered a term of great offence. Thus, for a Muslim, for one to infer that mankind could apprehend or understand *anything* about Allah's actual nature, or to even venture to question what the Qur'an says about Allah is a legally punishable offense.

Consequently, Muslim scholars do not speak of "theology" per se when dis-cussing Allah and the Qur'an. In fact Muslim scholars go to great lengths to avoid giving any appearance of speculating about the nature of Allah himself, while enabling doctrinal deliberations and decisions through what is termed as the disciplines of the Islamic Fields of Knowledge (Al-Ulum

---

4 Ravi Zacharias (Author and General Editor), ***Beyond Opinion: Living the Faith We Defend***. In Chapter 4 entitled "The Challenge from Islam" the writer, Sam Soloman, identifies and discusses four challenges, (1) Theological, (2) Political, (3) Administrative, and (4) Pragmatic. However he demon-strates that challenges 2, 3 and 4 emanate from the theological (1).

5 Allah reveals only his "will" in the form of instructions, commands, mandates, and imposed "cove-nants". (See references 5 and 6 in the Bibliography)

Al-Islamiyah), which include the Discipline of Morals (E'lm Al Akhlaq), the Discipline of Talk about Allah (E'lm Al-Kalam), and the Discipline of Jurisprudence (E'lm Al-Fiqh).[6]

However, we will be using the term "theology" for purposes of clarity as this book concerns itself entirely with the theological differences between the "unknowable Allah" and the self-revealing LORD God of the Judeo-Christian scriptures.

Regarding his nature, Allah "revealed" his 99 names/attributes. To the rational mind, this list would appear to be descriptions of Allah's "nature"—the very thing that is prohibited in Islam—and so is a classic example of a "contradiction in terms". But in fact, the undisputed Islamic doctrinal position of Islamic scholars down through time is that these 99 revealed "names/attributes" are *not* considered to refer to his "nature".

Yet some Christian theologians would differ and would refuse to accept the Islamically defined purpose of the names/attributes, and instead would accept them at face value as being bona fide descriptions of "Allah's nature", thus facilitating the use of these names/attributes to deduce a "sufficient similarity" with the attributes of the LORD God of the Bible for purposes of "bridging". As a result, without realizing it, or perhaps without knowing or taking into account what Islamic doctrine actually states and maintains (and what the Muslims really believe), in effect these theologians have lent credibility to an Islamic position of "sameness" and thus have unwittingly contributed to the undermining of the truth of the Bible.

It will be the task of this book to demonstrate systematically that these apparent similarities are neither true "similarities", much less "sufficient similarities", nor are they "misunderstandings" as the result of insufficient access to the Biblical scriptures. Instead, they are an intentional point-by-point countering of the entire Biblical narrative and the whole counsel of the Judeo-Christian scriptures.

---

6 This book will not delve into the details of these disciplines. However, relevant arguments from Islamic sources will be provided where applicable.

The Parallel Islamic Narrative

Since the Qur'an is not chronological—nor is it ordered in any productive or readily observable way—any comparison is a labor-intensive endeavor, which is further compounded and compromised, and in point of fact, even further obscured by the substantive incorporation throughout the text of significant Biblical names, doctrinal terms, geographic locations, and even familiar key historic events, giving the perception of being somewhat parallel with the Biblical account, yet with diametrically opposing characterizations and definitions.

Hence, rather than getting distracted at the outset with precisely "how" the Qur'an is ordered within its own historical context, we will defer an in-depth discussion of these equally critical aspects of Qur'anic textual order to Chapter 2, to keep the focus on delineating the nature, extent and impact of the incorporation and re-definition of Biblical elements within the text.

As stated earlier, the Qur'an starts out immediately by claiming "sameness" in regard to Allah and the LORD God. But it also lays claims to reflect "sameness" of revelation through a long list of (re-defined) Biblical prophets from Adam to Jesus, ending with Muhammad himself as the fulfillment of all previous prophecies, as well as full textual sameness through the alleged inclusion of the Torah, Psalms and Gospels, (renamed as, the Tawrat, Zaboor, and Injeel) as having "come down" from the "Eternal Tablet" that is the "Mother of the Book", the Qur'an.

It is difficult to say which is more egregious among such incorporated and redefined terminologies and characterizations—the claim of the entire (re-defined) timeline of revelation represented by appropriation of the pivotal Biblical characters and events? Or is it the bold claim to the title of "Creator"— whereby in one simultaneous and multi-faceted stroke, the nature of the LORD God is both equated with Allah and downgraded, or purged, to fit perfectly with the Islamic "Tawheed" by removing what Islam sees as "partners" or "associates", i.e. the Holy Spirit and Christ Jesus the Son of God.

In other words, embedded in the claim of "sameness", is the further tacit claim that the LORD God of the Biblical scriptures was *never* Triune in His nature, but was always detached, absolutely singular, and thus in line with the doctrine of "Islamic Monotheism", i.e. the "Tawheed".

Furthermore, in "correcting" the "Trinity" by purging or cleansing it of "partners", Muhammad has rendered it an absurdity to even consider the remote possibility that the God of the Universe could incarnate into human history.

Notwithstanding these stark realities about the nature of Allah, Islam, and Islamic Monotheism, in a superficial reading of the Qur'an, Allah seemingly appears like the LORD God of the scriptures, the God of creation who is also the sustainer, the preserver, and the provider for His creation. But the acid test is: If Allah were to be the same "creator", then his divine nature should be precisely the same, and thus his "creation" should both mirror and affirm the Genesis account.

If the same creator, what did Allah create?

When taking a closer look at the Qur'anic account of Allah's actual "creation", it becomes increasingly clear that what we are observing is a "creation" which may have the illusion, or surface trappings of the Genesis account, but which in detail and in core essence is quite different. Consequently, if the Qur'anic "creation" is different (on any level) from the Genesis account, it cannot be the handiwork of the LORD God of the Bible.

Notwithstanding this obvious and foundational difference, many Christian scholars who are looking for similarities/common ground all too easily accept the Islamic claim of Allah as the "creator god" on face value, rather than questioning in any depth the true nature and end result of Allah's "Creation".

This assumption of parity between the LORD God and Allah as "creator" leads to a virtual contagion of further misapprehensions and misconceptions down line by many Christian theologians, including the attribution of the Biblical concept of "general and special revelation" to the interpretation of the Qur'an. (Note: there is no concept of general and/or special revelation in Islam. Instead Islam speaks of Tanzil [coming down] and Wahy [Islamic Inspiration]).

So, in superimposing a Biblical "lens" on the Qur'an by actively seeking to find parallels, and similarities to base even further hopes on, the contagion proceeds to view the Islamic declaration of the "oneness of Allah", or "Islamic Monotheism/Tawheed" as a form of "general revelation" about the nature of God as derived (for one example) through the Qur'an's account of Ibrahim, the Muslim version of "Abraham", when he observed the failures of the "idols" of his society, and reasoned through watching the elements of nature, i.e. the stars, the moon and the sun; that the God of the universe could not be a created thing, but is "The Creator" and "deserves worship." Thus Ibrahim went through a reasoning process that at face value might sound akin to the Biblical concept of "general revelation." However, this is far from being the case, as will be elucidated in Chapter 4. As you will see, this incorrect perception is based on man's abilities to perceive rather than being a direct revelation from the LORD God as in the Bible and therefore does not take into account the fact that Allah never speaks directly to his people, but only through angels and messengers.

In the same vein, the Qur'an is seen by these scholars also to contain a form of "Special Revelation", based on the earlier mentioned incorporation within the Qur'an of versions of Biblical messengers, prophets, and events.

It is reasoned that this use of the Biblical lens regarding "revelation" furthers the hope of identifying some similarities or partial truth(s) within the Qur'an as a common ground to be deployed initially as a bridge when engaging Muslims, with the view to be later augmented with the fuller Biblical understanding of who the true God is.

This approach, or "model" of seeing Allah as an "unknown God" is incorrectly based on the Acts 17 model of the Mars Hill "unknown God". The aim is "meet them where they are", and to ultimately bring this purported "flawed" and faulty apprehension of "who Allah is" (according to Islam) into an expanded and corrected understanding of the true God of the Bible, by first accepting "assumed" common elements.

The trouble with this approach is that the "assumption" that Allah is an "unknown God" in the Qur'an is simply not the case. Instead, the Allah of the Qur'an is defined doctrinally, not as an "*unknown* God", but instead as an "*unknowable* God", in that he NEVER reveals his nature—and furthermore this self-prohibition is reinforced in the discipline of Islamic Jurisprudence (E'lm Al-Fiqh) with multiple layers of boundaries which serve to bar his followers from questioning on any level.

Therefore, the vast difference between the "unknown God" of the Mar's Hill passage represents a different mindset among the people of Athens toward "God" than that which is prescribed for followers of Islam, in that it is clear in this case that a god, such as Allah, who doesn't reveal himself will forever remain unknown and unknowable.

Compounding the error, these scholars, when making such comparisons side-step or place in abeyance the implications of the centrality and the uniqueness of Christ throughout the Biblical scriptures, as well as ignoring the other pivotal factors such as the historical progression (including the covenants) and typology-theology whereby everything in the scriptures speak of Christ. Whether it is the moral law, whether it is the ceremonial law, whether it is the temple, whether it is the prophets, whether it is the sacrifices—in fact, all of the scriptures—speak of Christ.

Typology: The Crimson Thread/Redemptive Analogies

We Christians believe in typology-theology, often called, typological symbolism, the Crimson Thread, the Redemptive Analogies, the Promise Plan of God, and/or others, each of being based on a hermeneutic which postulates that God placed foreshadows and promises of the coming of Christ in the laws, events, and people of the Old Testament.[7]

This belief says that:

- Adam was a foreshadow of Jesus[8] (man of dust/man of heaven),

- Abraham was a foreshadow of Jesus (father of faith, Gen 17; Isaiah 41:8),

- Isaac represented Jesus (sacrifice of son Gen 22:1-22),

- Joseph represented Jesus (suffering servant, Gen 37-50; Zechariah 11:13),

---

7 See for example References 17, 18, and 19 among others.

8 "[45] So it is written: 'The first man Adam became a living being'; the last Adam, a life-giving spirit. [46] The spiritual did not come first, but the natural, and after that the spiritual. [47] The first man was of the dust of the earth; the second man is of heaven. [48] As was the earthly man, so are those who are of the earth; and as is the heavenly man, so also are those who are of heaven. [49] And just as we have borne the image of the earthly man, so shall we bear the image of the heavenly man." 1 Cor. 15:45-49.

- Moses represented Jesus (the deliverer, Matt 2:15; Hosea 11:1),
- King David represented Jesus (King in exile, Rev 22:16; Isaiah 17:1-53, I Samuel 22:1-2)
- And much more.

In each of the above, the series of covenants—themselves foreshadows and typologies of Christ—were given and affirmed in succeeding generations. In so doing, the Biblical narrative emerges within historical context, reflecting the LORD God's self-revelation in creation, how He planned to redeem fallen mankind and how He promised a new covenant in Christ that would be "written on the heart", not on stone[9]. This New Covenant was fulfilled in Christ.[10]

This Christ-centered typology was the standard accepted Biblical hermeneutic as affirmed and taught by Jesus to his disciples, as well as by the early Church Fathers[11]. It was also uniformly confirmed by subsequent generations of theologians and church leaders up until around the 18th-19th centuries when, as a result of creeping societal changes, intellectual forces challenged traditional institutions like the Church, and emphasized reason, analysis, and individualism. Concurrently, due to the pragmatic shift in society, there was a related shift in scholarly emphasis within the seminaries to put the focus on the textual context of scripture—with the result that context took precedence over supernatural affirmations through types and foreshadowings.

These typological reflections of the promises leading to fulfillment were increasingly seen to depend too heavily on a God who is involved and present,

---

9 The New Covenant is prophesied in the Book of Jeremiah, "[31] 'Behold, the days are coming, declares the Lord, when I will make a new covenant with the house of Israel and the house of Judah, [32] not like the covenant that I made with their fathers on the day when I took them by the hand to bring them out of the land of Egypt, my covenant that they broke, though I was their husband, declares the Lord. [33] For this is the covenant that I will make with the house of Israel after those days, declares the Lord: I will put my law within them, and I will write it on their hearts. And I will be their God, and they shall be my people. [34] And no longer shall each one teach his neighbor and each his brother, saying, 'Know the Lord,' for they shall all know me, from the least of them to the greatest, declares the Lord. For I will forgive their iniquity, and I will remember their sin no more." Jer. 31:31-34. See also Ezek. 11:19-20, and 36:25-27, 37:27.

10 [16] "This *is* the covenant that I will make with them after those days, says the Lord: I will put My laws into their hearts, and in their minds I will write them," [17] *then He adds,* "Their sins and their lawless deeds I will remember no more." [18] Now where there is remission of these, *there is* no longer an offering for sin." Heb. 10:16. See also Heb. 9:15

11 With the notable exception of Marcion.

who gives a more direct divine guidance than was comfortable in the dawning age of "reason"[Ref. 7].

Another explanation for its partial demise was the lengths to which some scholars extended symbolic correlation down to the minute details of the Old Testament Jewish rituals and practices. Taken together, this problem was further compounded by the liberal trend to de-emphasize the "supernatural" or "allegorical", for fear of being accused of "finding Jesus under every rock." However, the place and relevance of typology within Biblical hermeneutics is irrefutable as it is based firmly on the scriptures themselves.

We have a clear and final validation coming not from the words of man, but from the very words of the risen Lord Jesus Christ following His resurrection, and prior to His ascension. As He walked, unrecognized as to who He was, with two of His disciples along the Emmaus Road, He engaged them about the events of the past few days in Jerusalem, and as they were voicing their disappointments regarding His crucifixion, He exhorted them as follows,

> (Luke 24:25-27), *"²⁵ He said to them, 'How foolish you are, and how slow to believe all that the prophets have spoken! ²⁶ Did not the Messiah have to suffer these things and then enter his glory?" ²⁷ And **beginning with Moses and all the Prophets, he explained to them what was said in all the Scriptures concerning himself.**'"*

Still, it was not until the risen Jesus accompanied them into the village, and accepted their invitation to dine did they recognize Him as their Lord.

Then He appeared to them as a group in Jerusalem while they were sharing their experiences of Him having earlier appeared to the two on the Emmaus Road,

> (Luke 24:44-48), *"⁴⁴ He said to them, 'This is what I told you while I was still with you: **Everything must be fulfilled that is written about me in the Law of Moses, the Prophets and the Psalms.**' ⁴⁵ Then he opened their minds so they could understand the Scriptures. ⁴⁶ He told them, 'This is what is written: The Messiah will suffer and rise from the dead on the third day, ⁴⁷ and repentance for the forgiveness of sins will be preached in his name to all nations, beginning at Jerusalem. ⁴⁸ You are witnesses of these things.'"*

Notwithstanding this compelling proof from our Lord in His own words, that indeed His incarnation, crucifixion, burial, resurrection and ascension were foreshadowed and prophesied in the Law, the Prophets and the Psalms—these typologies are all too often neglected, or in some cases intentionally minimized for the previously mentioned reasons, especially that of lack of favor for the "supernatural" and "allegorical" affirmations.

To further substantiate the point, here are a few New Testament references harking back to the Old Testament:

- Matt. 8:17, "...*that it might be fulfilled which was spoken by Isaiah the prophet, saying: 'He Himself took our infirmities And bore our sicknesses.'*"

- John 5:36-40, "*36 But I have a greater witness than John's; for the works which the Father has given Me to finish—the very works that I do—bear witness of Me, that the Father has sent Me. 37 And the Father Himself, who sent Me, has testified of Me. You have neither heard His voice at any time, nor seen His form. 38 But you do not have His word abiding in you, because whom He sent, Him you do not believe. 39 You search the Scriptures, for in them you think you have eternal life; and these are they which testify of Me.40 But you are not willing to come to Me that you may have life.*"

- 1 Cor. 10:4, "*... and all drank the same spiritual drink. For they drank of that spiritual Rock that followed them, and that Rock was Christ.*"

This passage is even more assertive when seen within its full context:

1 Cor. 10:1-4, "*1Moreover, brethren, I do not want you to be unaware that all our fathers were under the cloud, all passed through the sea, 2 all were baptized into Moses in the cloud and in the sea, 3 all ate the same spiritual food, 4 and all drank the same spiritual drink. For they drank of that spiritual Rock that followed them, and that Rock was Christ.*"

The Bible continues to emphasize that the "righteousness of God" is "revealed" by faith alone:

- Romans 1:17, "*For in it the righteousness of God is revealed from faith to faith; as it is written, 'The just shall live by faith.'*"

- Gal. 3:8, "*And the Scripture, foreseeing that God would justify the Gentiles by faith, **preached the gospel to Abraham beforehand**, saying, 'In you all the nations shall be blessed.'*"

- Gal. 3:16, "*The promises were spoken to Abraham and to his seed. Scripture does not say 'and to seeds,' meaning many people, but **'and to your seed,' meaning one person, who is Christ.***"

It is important to note that many Christian theologians and missiologists who work with Muslims have set aside or hesitated to make use of these typologies for yet another problematic reason—that is, because of the Qur'an's strong opposition to the deity of Christ, and the Muslims fear regarding the step of accepting Jesus as God—which the Qur'an attests is "making partners with Allah", and so is "idolatry", which is "Shirk", the unforgivable sin in the Qur'an[12]. Yet these same scholars have been pleased to employ the "similarities" between major Biblical figures and their apparent Qur'anic counterparts as "bridges to understanding", without taking into account—or perhaps without knowing—that these figures, from Adam to Jesus, not only have Islamized names in the Qur'an, they have Islamized personalities, purposes and messages.

Being drawn by the glitter of "sameness", they have created certain criteria which would vindicate their approach and methodologies, but at the expense of Biblical truths.

Little do they realize that they are buying into an intentional and very effective Islamic theme within the Qur'an of incorporating aspects of the Judeo-Christian scriptures that served to gain authority for Muhammad with the Meccean idol worshippers and a temporary but crucial validation from among the Jews and Christians of the day in Arabia—while at the same time becoming a mechanism to house very different doctrinal claims, all of which are in diametric opposition to the deity and salvific purposes of Christ.

---

12 "Surely, they have disbelieved who say: 'Allah is the Messiah [Issa, son of Maryam]'... Whosoever sets up partners in worship with Allah, then Allah has forbidden Paradise for him, and the Fire will be his abode. And for the unjust/polytheists there are no helpers." Surah 5:72

If This Be So, What Then?

In the light of the foregoing implications, to even begin to comprehend the Islamic concept of Allah as compared to the LORD God, we need to re-examine this dichotomy through an honest holistic process of compare/contrast between the two entities, rather than continue to hold to the "similarities only", or what some would term "sufficient similarities" criteria—which approach considers "differences" as an inconvenient misunderstanding that can be ameliorated with enough patience, forbearance, and love. "Differences" are viewed as causing conflict and discord, rather than being a valid attempt to discover the truth of the matter. Opting for similarities only, sufficient or not, is a call for "peace and harmony" at the expense of truth.

If, at the end of the day the Allah of Islam should differ to the extreme degree we posit, one must be prepared to put aside preconceived understandings, and favorite methodologies, as well as allegiances to proponents of current missiological practices based on these similarities—and take upon oneself the personal task of re-assessing this issue.

To that end, in approaching the Allah vs. LORD God dichotomy, at some point we need to identify and quantify exactly how and where Allah differs from the LORD God of the Bible and to what degree.

Chapter 2
The "Sameness" Claim Serves Multiple Purposes

The Logical Twist! The Same, and Not the Same, at the Same Time!

Now let's go deeper with the "sameness" façade, or illusion because it is this protected aura as articulated in the Qur'an, "...*our Allah and your Allah is one (the same)...*", which veils and protects the hidden identity of the true Allah from scrutiny.

Ironically, it is also this aura of "sameness"—when Qur'anic claims are *not found* to be substantiated within the pages of the Bible—that necessitates and facilitates Islamic charges of "corruption" against the "People of the Book", the Jews and the Christians. Having thus allegedly tampered with Allah's words, they are declared guilty of blasphemy, and therefore justifiably deserving of Allah's eternal wrath!

In the following two sections we provide the basis for this convoluted reasoning,

- First, the roots of the "sameness" claims in the Qur'an,

- Then, how this initial "sameness" claim at some point, inevitably necessitates the further Islamic claim of "Biblical corruption".

Later on, in the section on Biblical corruption, we provide illustrations whereby Islam attempts to support and justify this logic.

The Roots of the "Sameness" Illusion

As earlier stated, the source of the sameness claims being rooted from the outset in the Qur'an itself, upon further scrutiny can be seen to extend and penetrate both directly and indirectly past the Allah/LORD God dichotomy to undermine the doctrinal depths of Biblical Christianity.

The direct claims to sameness made in the Qur'an in the following select verses (Ayah's), at face value, give the distinct *appearance* of validating the Biblical account, as we see below in the first two phrases of Surah 29:46,

> *"And do not argue with the People of the Scripture except in a way that is best, except for those who commit injustice among them, and say, 'We believe in **that which has come down to us and had come down to you**; our Ilah (Allah) and your Ilah (God) is One', …"*

However, the true and full meaning of this complete passage becomes clearer in the third and final phrase of that Surah—which puts this claim of "sameness" within proper Islamic context,

> *"…and to him we have submitted (as Muslims)."*

Another translation of the same Ayah puts it this way, giving a better perspective of the *implications* of what is really being said—that rather than being an affirmation, it is a direct challenge:

> *"And dispute not with the People of the Book, except with means better than mere argument, unless it be with those of them who inflict wrong, but say, 'We believe in the revelation which has **come down to us and in that which came down to you; Our Allah and your Allah is one; and it is to him we bow (in Islam).**'"*

The official Islamic commentary (Tafsir Al-Jalalayn) draws out these implications explicitly. It states,

> *"And do not dispute with the People of the Scripture unless it be in that manner of disputation, bettering the most virtuous way, such as calling [them] to Allah by [reference to] His signs and pointing out His arguments; except [in the case of] those of them who have done wrong, by waging war and refusing to accept [to pay] the jizya-tax: dispute with these using the sword, until such time as they submit or pay the jizya-tax; **and say, to those who have accepted [the imposition upon them of] the jizya-tax, should they inform you of something stated in their Scriptures: 'We believe in that which has been revealed to us and revealed to you — and neither believe nor disbelieve them in that [which they tell you] — our Allah and your God is one [and the same], and to Him we submit as Muslims'.**"[13]*

---

[13] http://www.altafsir.com/Tafasir.asp?tMadhNo=0&tTafsirNo=74&tSoraNo=29&tA-yahNo=46&tDisplay=yes&UserProfile=0&LanguageId=2

In other words this commentary explains that this passage, rather than being an affirmation, on the contrary is actually an explicit challenge to the "People of the Book" to search their scriptures, whereby they would discover that indeed, Allah and the God of their Bible are the same.

Note that this verse (Ayah) goes far beyond the single claim to the alleged "sameness" of Allah and the LORD God, to further infer that the entire textual content of the Biblical "revelation" is also the same as the textual content of the Qur'an.

The following two Surah's (among many others) explicitly confirm and establish the assertion of textual identity between the Qur'an and the Judeo-Christian scriptures:

> Meccean Surah 10:37, "*And this Qur'an is not such as could ever be produced by other than Allah, but it is a **confirmation of which was before it**[14], and a full explanation of the Book[15] - wherein there is no doubt from the Lord of the worlds (i.e. all that Allah has created, such as the angels, Jinn and humans)."*

> Medina Surah 3:3, "*It is he (Allah) who has sent down the Book to you (i.e. Muhammad) with truth, **confirming what came before it**. And he sent down the Tawrat and the Injeel."*

But it doesn't stop there, according to the earlier passage in Surah 29:46, which is repeated here for emphasis and clarity:

> "… '*We believe in **that which has been revealed to us and has been revealed to you**; our Ilah (Allah) and your Ilah (God) is One*', with the completing phrase "*…and to Him we have submitted as Muslims."*

Therefore, this key Surah represents not one or two, but a virtual set of claims which, each in turn encompass the entire scope of the Judeo-Christian scriptures, including the full range of revelation, from general to special. The effect is to counter Biblical accounts of the Creator and His creation; the nature of mankind and their relationship to the Creator; the prophets/messengers and

---

14 Meaning the earlier books that came down from the Eternal Tablet, such as the Tawrat, Zaboor and Injeel.
15 Meaning, the Qur'an.

their roles; the historical/doctrinal narrative; the Biblical message, and finally, the ultimate salvific/apocalyptic outcome.

In other words, this one sentence in Surah 29:46 (as confirmed in Surah's 10:37 and 3:3), encapsulates and reflects the sweeping Qur'anic claim to counter the whole counsel of the Judeo-Christian scriptures—point by point.

Hence, we need to meticulously examine every aspect and nuance of each of the stated or inferred Qur'anic claims to *sameness*, starting with *"…Our Allah and your Allah is one…"*

The Qur'anic Call "back" to "Islamic Monotheism"

This Qur'anic "call" claims to hark back in history to "affirm" and "correct" previous revelations as we saw in Surah 29:46 earlier, and now also in the first part of Surah 3:84 to follow:

> *"…Say, (Muhammad), 'we have believed in Allah and what* ***came down*** *to us, and what* ***came down*** *to Ibrahim (Abraham), Ismaeel (Ishmael), Is-haq (Isaac), Yacoub (Jacob), and the tribes, and in what* ***was given*** *to Moosa (Moses) and Issa (Jesus), and to the prophets from their Lord. We make no distinction amongst them, and to him (Allah) we are Muslims".*

Once more we see that while initially giving the appearance of "affirming" the Biblical record in the first part of the verse above, the concluding phrase of that verse, i.e. *"… and to him (Allah) we are Muslims,"* amends the identity of all these Biblical prophets/messengers to have been Muslims.

So here we see another example that the Qur'an both "affirms", and modifies (or corrects) the Biblical account simultaneously. To sum up, we have seen an emerging motif of:

- The repeating claim to sameness between the Allah of the Qur'an and the LORD God of the Bible,
- The repeating claim of the sameness of the prophets and their messages.
- The repeating claim to sameness between the texts.

Next we go into the details of the claims of sameness of the texts.

Claim to Textual Sameness Expressed Visually in the Eternal Tablet

As one can see, this claim to textual identity is rooted in the Qur'an and visually expressed in the "Eternal Tablet", i.e. the "Mother of the book", the original Qur'an, as mentioned in the above verse, and as pictured below in Figure 1 whereby all revealed scriptures (including the Tawrat, the Zaboor, and the Injeel)"came down" from the same source.

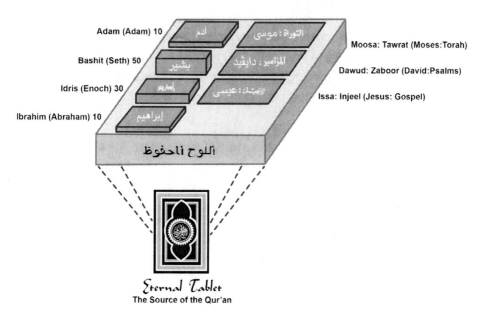

Eternal Tablet
The Source of the Qur'an

Figure 1: The Eternal Tablet is given in Surah 85:21-22 "21. This is a Glorious Qur'an, 22. inscribed in The Preserved Tablet (Al-Lauh Al-Mahfuz)".

This tablet is said to have "come down" from the highest heaven to the lowest heaven. It is said to have contained all of the holy books (including the Bible) without exception, so it can be seen that the Islamic view is that all previous holy books were but early and partial installments, i.e. "early editions" of the eternal Qur'an.

This figure illustrates the Islamic doctrine that different portions of the "Eternal Tablet" were given incrementally over time to various prophets starting with the Biblical characters/prophets and culminating with Muhammad as the "Seal of the Prophets".[16]

---

16 The entire process of transmission of divine revelations from the Eternal Tablet to the various prophets/messengers using the intermediary actions of angelic beings, such as Jibril (Qur'anic version of Biblical Gabriel) is given in Chapter 3 below.

Now, it is claimed that the first 100 books have been lifted back up and the relevant material that remains applicable and needed by mankind has been incorporated into the current Qur'an. So the 100 books of the 104 on the Tablet in this illustration are untraceable. However, the remaining 3 (i.e. Tawrat, Zaboor and Injeel) out of 4, are said to have been left behind as these three allegedly still speak of Muhammad in a detailed manner—and therefore serve as a current form of "testimony" to the validity of Muhammad.

Consequently, with the coming of the current Qur'an all of the earlier books have become irrelevant. Their only purpose was (and is) to attest to the announcement of the message and mission of Muhammad as the Seal of the Prophets. As such—as having now been superseded—their content is irrelevant to a Muslim.

The concept of "lifting up" or "taking back" is related to the absolute authority of Allah as the author and possessor of the Mother of the book, meaning the "Eternal Tablet." Hence, the concept of "for every age or period, there is a book" according to Surah 13:38-39,

> "*We did send messengers before you, and appointed for them wives and children: and it was never the part of a messenger to bring a sign except with Allah's permission. **For each period is a Book**. Allah blots out and establishes what he wishes, and with him is the Mother of the Book, (i.e. the Eternal Tablet/Qur'an)*"

Content of the 104 "Books" that "Came Down"

The Qur'anic reference to the actual content of other scriptures/revelations, or "books" which "came down" from the Tablet to messengers or prophets from Adam to Issa (Books 1-103), prior to Muhammad's "call" (resulting in the current Qur'an, book 104) is scanty regarding events, or their mission and purposes other than by inference —with the following critical exceptions—which themselves include considerable further embedded enigmatic "inferences", when read carefully, all "bearing witness" to the following:

1) Muhammad's "coming" and mission: All the 103 books and the prophets preceding Muhammad are claimed to have borne witness to Allah's imposed "covenant", termed "The Covenant of the Prophets". This imposed covenant announced the future "coming" of the

"expected one", i.e. Muhammad, as well as a specific definition of his mission "to confirm what you have" (meaning in particular, the Tawrat, Zaboor, and Injil).

> Surah 3:81 states, "*Behold! Allah took the **covenant of the prophets**, saying: 'I give you a book and wisdom; then comes to you a **messenger, confirming what is with you**; do you **believe in him** and **render him help**.' Allah said: 'Do you agree, and take this my Covenant as binding on you?' They said: 'We agree.' He said: 'Then bear witness, and I am with you among the witnesses.' "*

Although the term "covenant" is frequently used in the Qur'an it is not a covenant in the Biblical sense. Instead it conveys a unilateral imposition by Allah with no reciprocity.

Hence the "Covenant of the Prophets" in Surah 3:81 is an imposed "covenant" requiring no obligations on the part of Allah toward his creation, but simply announcing and instituting the terms of "submission" which were required of all the prophets in regard to the predicted future "coming" of Muhammad—that they would expect him, and that they would "agree" in advance to accept him, to "believe him" and to "aid him" when he comes and with Allah acting as a "witness" to his own imposition.

2) The prophets/messengers all bore witness of their own identity as being "Muslim".

3) The prophets/messengers all bore witness as having personally preached "Islam" to their respective peoples.

Following are some key examples confirming these three points:

- Surah 2:136, "*Say (O Muslims), '**We believe in Allah and that which has been sent down to us and that which has been sent down to Ibrahim (Abraham), Ismaeel (Ishmael), Is-haq (Isaac), Ya'qub (Jacob), and to the Tribes, and that which has been given to Moosa (Moses) and Issa (Jesus), and that which has been given to the prophets from their Lord. We make no distinction between any of them, and to him (i.e. Allah) we are Muslims.**'"*

33

- Surah 3:84, "*Say (O Muhammad): 'We believe in Allah and in what has been sent down to us, and what was sent down to Ibrahim (Abraham), Ismaeel (Ishmael), Is-haq (Isaac), Ya'qub (Jacob) and the tribes, and what was given to Moosa (Moses), Issa (Jesus) and the prophets from their Lord. We make no distinction between them **and to him we are Muslims.**'*"

- Surah 10:72, "*And if you turn away then no payment have I asked of you. My reward is only from Allah, and I (i.e. Nooh) **have been commanded to be of the Muslims.**"*

- Surah 3:67, "***Ibrahim** was neither a Jew nor a Christian, but he **was a Hanafi Muslim**. And he was not of the polytheists.*"

- Surah 2:130, "*And who would be averse to the **religion of Ibrahim** (i.e. Islam) except one who makes a fool of himself ...*"

- Surah 2:131, "*When his Lord said to **him** (i.e. Ibrahim), '**Submit as a Muslim**', he said '**I have submitted in Islam** to the Lord of the worlds.'*"

- Surah 2:133, "*Or were you witnesses when death approached **Ya'qub(Jacob)**, when he said to his sons, 'Who will you worship after me?' They said, 'We will worship your God and the God of your fathers, **Ibrahim and Ismaeel and Is-haq- one god. And to him we are Muslims.**'*"

- Surah 10:84, "*And **Moosa** said, '**O my people**, if you have believed in Allah, then rely upon him, **if you are Muslims.**'*"

- Surah 12:101, "*My Lord, You have given **me (i.e. Yusuf)** sovereignty and taught me of the interpretation of dreams. Creator of the heavens and earth, you are my protector in this world and in the hereafter. **Cause me to die a Muslim...**"*

- Surah 5:111, "*And as I inspired **the disciples (of Issa)**, 'Believe in me and in my messenger Issa.' They said, 'We have believed, **so bear witness that indeed we are Muslims.**'*"

Note carefully the wording of the above key Qur'anic Surah's, claiming a "Muslim" identity with/for all of the Biblical prophets (as well as the disciples of Jesus), and thus inferring that the entire text itself has been "sent down" from the Eternal Tablet.

Below are the listings of the specific "books" that were allegedly "sent down" to each of the presumably Muslim prophets:

- Biblical Adam: Muslim name is also Adam. Given 10 books that "came down" from the tablet, *but only <u>one</u> prophesy*...the coming of Muhammad!

- Biblical Seth: Muslim name is Bashit. Given 50 books that "came down" from the tablet, *but only <u>one</u> prophesy*...the coming of Muhammad!

- Biblical Enoch: Muslim name is Idris. Given 30 books that "came down" from the tablet, *but only <u>one</u> prophesy*...the coming of Muhammad!

- Biblical Abraham: Muslim name is Ibrahim. Given 10 books that "came down" from the tablet, *but only <u>one</u> prophesy*...the coming of Muhammad!

- Biblical Moses: Muslim name is Moosa. Given 1 book, the (Torah) Tawrat that "came down" from the tablet, *but only <u>one</u> prophesy*... the coming of Muhammad!

- Biblical David: Muslim name is Dawood. Given 1 book, the (Psalms) Zaboor that "came down" from the tablet, *but only <u>one</u> prophesy*...the coming of Muhammad!

Biblical Jesus: Muslim name is Issa. Given 1 book, the (Gospel) Injeel that "came down" from the tablet, *but only <u>one</u> prophesy*...the coming of Muhammad! In short, all the reconstructed Biblical characters mentioned in the Qur'an—without exception—testified to being "Muslim", preaching "Islam", and each one prophesied only a single prophesy, which is: *"The promise of the "good tidings" of the "expected one" Ahmad (one of Muhammad's names)."*

> Surah 61:6, *"And as, Issa, the son of Maryam, said: 'O Children of Israel, I am the messenger of Allah sent to you, confirming the Tawrat (Torah, or Law) before me, and giving* **glad tidings of a messenger to come after me, whose name shall be Ahmad**[17]*...'"*

---

17 Ahmad is one of the names of Muhammad, as it is one of the derivative names from the same root.

The Sameness Claim Does Double Duty: It Masks Profound "Differences", and Necessitates the Charges of Biblical Corruption

What Happens when Texts Do Not Match?

The underlying assumption of the foregoing issue of sameness relates to the Islamic assertion that the original texts of the Torah (Tawrat), Psalms (Zaboor) and Gospel (Injeel) *should* contain the same textual content as is found in the Qur'an—as all these books have allegedly emanated from the "Eternal Tablet"(i.e. the Qur'an), and hence from the same deity.

However, in reality the Judeo-Christian scriptures stand in content and concept completely different and contradictory to the Qur'an including facts, events, doctrines, as well as the entire narrative and its theological implications.

Hence, the Islamic position towards what we have in our hands as the "Bible" is that it is nothing but a tampered with and corrupted version of what originally "came down" from the Eternal Tablet.

These Qur'anic assertions underline and bolster the supremacy of Muhammad and his alleged role as a fulfillment of various prophecies within the Judeo-Christian scriptures. Neither Muhammad nor any of his followers, nor anyone anywhere, ever produced or claimed to produce original texts to substantiate this claim. Yet, the undisputed doctrinal position of the Qur'an is that the Bible has been tampered with by the Jews and the Christians, so as to render it corrupted[18] and no longer reliable, as affirmed unanimously by Muslim scholars.

Despite this, many Christians assert that the Qur'an itself does not claim Biblical corruption—but that it is just the Muslim scholars who do so. They are wrong on both counts, as we shall demonstrate.

---

18   http://islamqa.info/en/2001/http://islamqa.info/en/197537

Islamic Positions on Biblical Corruption

As a result, we are compelled to cover this issue in two parts.

First, we demonstrate that those Christians, who take the position that the Qur'an *does not claim* the corruption of the Bible, have misunderstood some of the central doctrines (Aqeeda's) of Islam regarding the "content" of the earlier revelations (i.e. the Tawrat and Injeel) on this issue.

Second, we detail and classify the full scope of Islamic doctrines on Biblical corruption as reported throughout the Qur'an.

How Could the Qur'an Possibly "Validate" the Judeo-Christian Scriptures?

Christian Scholars Position

Even with the above undisputed position of the Islamic scholars in view, many Christian scholars still maintain the incorrect position that the Qur'an *does NOT claim* Biblical corruption, but instead go further to erroneously conclude that the Qur'an actually *affirms* the authenticity of the Biblical text.

Due to the expediency policy of Muhammad to appease his audience, he would claim a revelation and then appropriately abrogate it in due time. Being unaware of what is abrogated and what is not, one tends to read the Qur'an at face value. Hence, this argument against "Biblical corruption" in the Qur'an is accepted and used in the development of missiological methodologies to attract Muslims to the Biblical scriptures. Aside from being based on wrong missiological assumptions, Muslims who are given such arguments can easily inquire of their Imams and scholars as to the reality behind such Qur'anic interpretations. The missionary who is given instructions to use such arguments enters as a result into a double bind: (a) Showing ignorance of Qur'anic concepts/teachings which will inevitably be corrected by the Imam, and (b) as a consequence causing the Muslims to further mistrust the missionary!

To substantiate the Christian scholars position, the following select Qur'anic Surah's are cited, but out of context: 10:94, 5:44, 5:46 and 5:68 among others. Taking these Surah's on face value without being aware of contextual considerations to be detailed below, one can see how such misconceptions could arise.

- Surah 10:94, "*So if you (Muhammad) are in doubt concerning that which we have revealed unto you, then ask those who are reading the Book before you. The truth has come to you from your Lord. So be not of those who doubt.*"

- Surah 5:44, "*Indeed, we sent down the Tawrat (Torah), in which was guidance and light. The prophets who submitted [to Allah] judged by it for the Jews, as did the rabbis and scholars by that with which they were entrusted of the Scripture of Allah, and they were witnesses thereto …*".

- Surah 5:46, "*And we sent, following in their footsteps, Issa son of Maryam, confirming that which came before him in the Tawrat; and we gave him the Injeel, in which was guidance and light and confirming that which preceded it of the Tawrat as guidance and instruction for the righteous.*"

- Surah 5:68, "*Say (Muhammad): 'O People of the Book, you have no ground to stand upon unless you stand fast by the Tawrat, the Injeel, and all the revelation that has come to you from your Lord.' It is the revelation that comes to you from your Lord, that increases in most of them their obstinate rebellion and blasphemy. But sorrow not (O Muhammad) over people who are without faith'*".

Before delving into the specifics of the contextual considerations in regard to the above Surah's, we need to step back and explain their exegesis as stated and expounded by Muslim scholars themselves within the discipline of Islamic interpretation of the Qur'an, termed "Tafsir."

How Some Christian Scholars Missed the Central Point

In the attempts by these Christian scholars to use such Surah's as 10:94, 5:44, 5:46 and 5:68 (as quoted above), at apparent "face value" in the Western sense, they have missed the actual meaning.

Considering Surah 10:94 which states,

> "*So if you (Muhammad) are in doubt concerning that which we have revealed unto you, then ask those who are reading the book before you, the truth has come to you from your Lord. So be not of those who doubt.*"

These Christian scholars have used this verse to base their argument on the superficial assumption that Muhammad must have had some doubts regarding the validity of the Qur'anic revelations which he claimed to be receiving, and that he was then directed by Allah himself (through Islamic inspiration, called Wahy) to verify the validity of his mission by seeking the confirmation from those of the Jews and Christians who knew their own scriptures well. This would, to them, then apparently provide ample evidence that Muhammad fully trusted the Judeo-Christian scriptures and found no reason to doubt their correctness and validity. But the truth of the matter is quite to the contrary!

It is the undisputed fact that all Muslim scholars and expositors of the Qur'an across the full spectrum maintain that *Muhammad is recorded, predicted and prophesied throughout the Judeo-Christian scriptures.*

Therefore, rather than affirming the Biblical text as a standard, this passage in Surah 10:94 is held by all Muslim scholars without exception as directing Muhammad to ask and enquire of the "People of the Book" regarding these prophecies confirming himself as the expected one and fulfillment of their scriptures.[19] In other words, this passage is seen as a strong admonition to Muhammad by Allah to hold the Christians and Jews accountable for these alleged prophecies.

In fact, Muhammad acted many times on the above admonition to confront and hold the "People of the Book" accountable for these assumed "prophecies within their own scriptures" about himself. Many such instances occurred while still in Mecca, but his first known application of this principle with physical consequences occurred in Medina when he faced down the first Jewish tribe (Banu Qaynuqa[20]) causing them to be expelled following a series of disagreements when he finally put them to the test by insisting that they acknowledge the existence of detailed prophecies about himself as the fulfillment of their scriptures.

---

[19] See http://www.altafsir.com/Tafasir.asp?tMadhNo=1&tTafsirNo=1&tSoraNo=10&tA-yahNo=94&tDisplay=yes&UserProfile=0&LanguageId=1 for the commentaries/expositions on this Surah (10:94) by Islamic scholars of all schools across the board affirming what is stated herein.
[20] See for example the Wikipedia account https://en.wikipedia.org/wiki/Banu_Qaynuqa and also Ref. (6)

This precedent was applied further in his dealing with the remaining Jews in Medina and beyond, and later the Christians of greater Arabia—up to the point when he developed and instituted a legal system whereby the "People of the Book" could remain in their "religion", but under severe constraints spelled out in a strict legal code known as "People of Obligation", i.e. Dhimmitude. However, the principle expressed in the Surah above that Christians and Jews must always be held accountable for the prophecies about Muhammad that they allegedly have in their own scriptures remains looming in the background to this day—whether or not it is acted upon physically or politically, especially when Christian and Jewish populations are under the auspices of an Islamic government and/or Islamic systems.

Now in the next Surah 5:44 Christian scholars have assumed (reasonably enough) that the "Tawrat" that is being referenced is nothing but the Pentateuch of the Old Testament and that Muhammad is directing his people to follow its teachings. But taken within Qur'anic context, this is far from being the case.

> Surah 5:44 states, "*Indeed, we sent down the Tawrat, in which was guidance and light. The prophets who submitted, judged by it for the Jews, as did the rabbis and scholars by that with which they were entrusted of the Scripture of Allah, and they were witnesses thereto …*".

Regarding the English translation aspect, a direct word-for-word translation is not sufficient, since the intended meaning by the Qur'anic texts require professional Islamic exegesis. Remember that as stated earlier, the same or similar terms as those in the Bible are used in the Qur'an but with different meanings. Therefore, a translation which is consistent with the exegesis (Tafsir) of the Muslim scholars, would look like this (with their summary explanations between parentheses and in bold):

> Surah 5:44 with explanatory phrases from the Tafsir, "*Indeed, we sent down the Tawrat (**the earlier limited version of the Qur'an from the Eternal Tablet**), in which was guidance and light (**i.e. Islam**). The prophets who **became Muslims** judged by it for the Jews, as did the rabbis and scholars by that with which they were entrusted of the Scripture of Allah (**i.e. whatever they received from the Eternal Tablet**), and they were witnesses thereto …*".

Note the following: The "Tawrat" being referred to herein is the "earlier limited version of the Qur'an from the Eternal Tablet." The term "guidance and light" is unanimously interpreted by Muslim Scholars as referring to "Islam", even during the time of the (Islamized) Patriarchs before Muhammad arrived on the scene. The earlier (Islamized) prophets who used the "Tawrat" to judge were already "Muslims". The exact Arabic here is "Wa Aslamu" i.e. they had embraced Islam. And finally the "Scripture of Allah" which they bore witness to was "from the Eternal Tablet"—i.e. the earlier limited version of the Qur'an as previously referenced.

To explain the position of Muslim scholars regarding the mission of Issa (The Qur'anic version of Jesus) in Surah 5:46, we have inserted (in bold) explanatory phrases which reflect the intended meanings:

> Surah 5:46, "*And we sent, following in their footsteps, Issa son of Maryam, confirming that which came before him in the Tawrat* **(the earlier limited version of the Qur'an from the Eternal Tablet)***; and we gave him the Injeel* **(the later limited version of the Qur'an from the Eternal Tablet)***, in which was guidance and light* **(i.e. Islam)** *and confirming that which preceded it of the Tawrat as guidance and instruction for the righteous***(pious).***"*

What the Qur'an is actually saying, is that the mission of Issa was to confirm the "Tawrat" which is seen as the "*earlier* limited version of the Qur'an", and was given the Injeel, which is then seen as the "*later* limited version of the Qur'an", both having emanated from the Eternal Tablet, and thus being "guidance and light" of Islam.

As for the "*reasons of the revelation*"[21] aspect of 5:46, it was revealed as a definitive answer to the purported "false claims" of both the Jews and the Christians of Muhammad's time. Muhammad said that all the prophets were Muslims. The Jews said, "No, they were not. They were Jews." While the Christians said that although the prophets were ethnically Jews, technically they were Christians, as they were all seen to be forerunners of Christ pointing to Christ. However, Allah "revealed" to Muhammad that they were neither, but that they were all Muslims and thus all witnesses of Muhammad.

---

[21] Called "Asbab Annuzul" in Arabic. It refers to the particular circumstance that necessitated a particular verse or a section of the Qur'an to be given to Muhammad.

According to the Islamic discipline of interpretation (Tafsir), Surah's 10:94, 5:44, 5:46, and 5:68, formulate and substantiate an Islamic doctrine (i.e. Aqeedah). As such all of these Surah's are regarded as fundamental (i.e. Muhkamat[22]). The doctrine being that the revelations given before (Tawrat and Injeel) were at the time and should be today completely compatible with what was given to Muhammad. The implication is that should it differ, then it must have been tampered with—pointing to Biblical corruption, and hence cannot be used.

But, surprisingly some Christian theologians refer in particular to Surah 5:68 as a conclusive proof of the endorsement and acceptability of the validity of the Judeo-Christian scriptures by the Qur'an. However, with a closer look at Surah 5:68, it becomes clear beyond a shadow of a doubt that this is not what the Surah is stating.

> Surah 5:68 states, "*Say (O Muhammad): 'O People of the Book you have no ground to stand upon unless you stand fast by the Tawrat, the Injeel, and all the revelation that has come to you from your Lord.' It is the revelation that comes to you from your Lord, that increases in most of them their obstinate rebellion and blasphemy. But do not sorrow (O Muhammad) over the blasphemous people'*".

Let's examine this verse from the Islamic position, by understanding the exegesis and the exposition of it by the Muslim scholars themselves. It is thus necessary to look at context and to break down this verse into phrases to comprehend its message and meaning:

(a) The context is that the Jews and the Christians are saying to Muhammad that their scriptures are valid. He, meaning Allah, responded by declaring "*Say (O Muhammad) 'O People of the Book you have no ground to stand on.*" Meaning your claims and defenses of your scripture is futile and you have no ground to stand on, i.e. meaning, until

---

22 In the Islamic commentaries (Tafsir) Qur'anic verses have various classifications. The Muhkamat verses, as opposed to the Mutashbihat (allegorical) ones are fully confirmed and eternal, as per Surah 3:7, "*It is he who has sent down to you (Muhammad) the book (Qur'an). In it are verses that are **entirely clear (Muhkamat)**, they are the foundations of the book **and others allegorical (Mutashbbihat)**...*"

you establish what has been revealed to you in the Tawrat and the Injeel (referring to the prophecies and predictions about Muhammad which had been recorded by name in your scriptures, to embrace him, to follow him, and to honor him).

(b) "... *that increases in most of them their obstinate rebellion and blasphemy*...": Meaning cease from rebellion and quit from being blasphemers.

(c) " ... *But do not sorrow (O Muhammad) over the blasphemous people*...": Meaning, O' Muhammad, let their rebellion and apostasy sadden you not.

Even more explicitly, Tafsir Al-Jalalayn gives this equivalent interpretation of Surah 5:68[23]:

"*Say: 'O People of the Scripture, you have no basis, in religion, on which to rely, until you observe the Tawrat and the Injeel and what was revealed to you from your Lord', by implementing what is therein, including believing in me [Muhammad]. And what has been revealed to you from your Lord, of the Qur'an, will surely increase many of them in insolence and disbelief, because of their disbelief in it; so do not grieve for the disbelieving folk, if they do not believe in you, in other words, do not be concerned with them.*"

Summary Regarding the Position of Some Christian Scholars

In short, the Islamic interpretation is that the "People of the Book" must "stand" by the original Tawrat and the Injeel which came down from the Eternal Tablet in accepting Muhammad, accepting his teachings and accepting the totality of Islam.

This is a stern rebuke and warning to the People of Book to abide by the teachings of Islam, by accepting him, Muhammad, as the "expected prophet" as per their scriptures and to cease and desist from adding anything to their scriptures as given to them originally from the Eternal Tablet (rejection of which is considered total blasphemy [Kufr]).

---

[23] Tafsir Al-Jalalayn on the Islamic interpretation of Surah 5:68 (http://www.altafsir.com/Tafasir. asp?tMadhNo=0&tTafsirNo=74&tSoraNo=5&tAyahNo=68&tDisplay=yes&UserProfile= 0&LanguageId=2

So, these verses are definitively *not* proof of the Qur'an having testified to the validity and soundness of the Judeo-Christian scriptures—as held by some Christian theologians—whereas in fact, they are testifying to the exact opposite.

Hence according to Islam, the Bible as we have it in our hands is characterized within the Qur'an as being corrupt, unreliable and untrustworthy.

The Qur'anic Charges of Definitive Corruption of the Biblical Scriptures: "Tahreef"

Having addressed the misguided position of some Christian scholars that the Qur'an affirms the Biblical text, we turn our attention in more detail to the official Islamic position on Biblical corruption.

The official Islamic position has a name, and that name represents a central doctrine of core Islam—it is called the "Doctrine of Tahreef".

Tahreef comes from the root word "Harf." Harf simply means, letter. Harrafa means distorted or when a letter is misplaced or substituted deliberately. So Tahreef is the act of misplacing or substituting letters to obscure, confuse or change the meaning.

Tahreef is a Qur'anic concept expressed as an Islamic doctrine. This doctrine goes hand in hand with the doctrine of "Wahy" (Islamic inspiration) and the "infallibility of the Qur'an," as per Surah 15:9, "*It is we who have revealed the remembrance (Dhikr, i.e. Qur'an), and assuredly we will preserve it. (eternally from corruption).*" According to Muslim scholars this protection is exclusively applied to the Qur'an only—hence, its application is eternal.

The numerous Qur'anic charges/allegations against the Bible came in varying degrees, both explicit and implicit—some by inference, others by deduction—with the foundational charge being a melding, or combination of direct, indirect, and inferential.

For the sake of clarity we have grouped these allegations into five categories. The first four are easier to demonstrate, so that an understanding of what they mean and how they were applied is necessary in order to grasp the wider scope of the fifth, or foundational charge from which they all emanate. Interestingly, it is this final charge that has been severely misunderstood and misapplied as being a limited and simplistic form of verbal distortion which would not affect the text, although in reality it is this charge that validates and upholds the other charges. These five charges are:

1. Corruption through omission and concealment

2. Corruption through falsification of events and doctrines

3. Corruption through making false claims about Allah and his prophets

4. Corruption by rewriting their own book and claiming or attributing its authorship to Allah

5. Corruption through distortion of the book and twisting of the tongue

These are now discussed in some detail with illustrations from the Qur'an itself.

1. Corruption through Omission and Concealment

The foundational charge of the omission and concealment accusations against the Bible by the Qur'an is that Muhammad is said to have been predicted and prophesied throughout the Biblical scriptures stating his name, as well as detailed descriptions of his person, and character. Since in reality there is no mention whatsoever of Muhammad in the Biblical scriptures, Muslims the world over believe without question the Qur'anic claim that the Bible has been tampered with.

A Muslim will ask such typical questions: "Is Muhammad mentioned or prophesied in your Bible?" Or, "Is his description mentioned?"

Here are some instances of explicit charges:

(a) Corruption by omission:

- Surah 61:6, "*And (remember) when Issa (Jesus), son of Maryam (Mary), said: "O Children of Israel! I am the messenger of Allah unto you confirming the Tawrat (Torah) which came before me, and **giving glad tidings of a messenger to come after me, whose name shall be Ahmad** ..."*"

- Surah 7:157, "*Those who follow the messenger, the illiterate prophet (i.e. Muhammad)* **whom they find written with them in the Tawrat (Torah) and the Injeel (Gospel)...**"

(b) Corruption by explicit concealment:

- Surah 2:146 "*Those to whom we gave the scripture (Jews and Christians) .... But a party of* **them conceal the truth while they know it.**"

- Surah 6:20 "*Those to whom we have given the scripture (Jews and Christians)* **recognize him (i.e. Muhammad) as they recognize their own sons...**"

2. Corruption through Falsification of Events and Doctrines

To comprehend this section, one would need to bear in mind that the order is in reverse, such that the Qur'an first "corrects" the Biblical accounts of events, doctrines, people, and places, and in so doing "recasts" them. Having changed the Biblical scriptures under the guise of "correction"—it then brings a charge against the Bible itself—a charge of "falsification by default", since it is clear that now the two accounts do not match.

These "corrections" are not random, but each and every one of them has an objective behind it. The overall objective is bigger than the variations in its details, for the sum of it all is a dual and simultaneous process to undo the knowability of God, the mission of Judeo-Christian scriptures as a whole, and particularly its culmination through Christ Jesus, the Word incarnate. The ultimate aim is to substantiate the authority and the finality of Muhammad as the "Seal of the Prophets" and Islam as the religion of Allah. But as these "corrected" verses are scattered all over the Qur'an with no chronological order, this process is somewhat veiled, and thus not immediately evident. Nevertheless it is there.

Hence we see that Muhammad DID bring something "new". Through the process of "correction", as explained above, he brought a "new narrative" with "new doctrines", "new goals" and "new outcomes"—all in the expressed intent of "going back" to the "original" Islamic monotheism that was "brought down" to the Christians and Jews from the Eternal Tablet. And then in charging the Christians and Jews with "corruption" because of his own "corrections", he deflected and gave the impression that he was "restoring" what was "lost" through "unfaithful stewards".

Typically, a Muslim would ask, "Was Jesus crucified? Is Jesus God? Did man sin? Did the devil tempt Jesus (especially since in Islam every child is pricked in his right rib by the devil at birth, and hence everyone would be tempted by the devil, with the exception of Issa)".[24]

In this section we record examples of events whereby the Qur'anic version is at complete variance with the Biblical one. Although the Qur'an came on the scene many hundreds of years after the Bible, we are told that the Qur'anic version is the true one and the Biblical one as false.

The Qur'an claims to be a "divine revelation" whereby Muhammad's own claim was that his recitation of the Qur'an, attested to his calling, according to Surah 12:3,

> *"We relate to you, [O Muhammad], the best of stories in what we have revealed to you of this Qur'an although you were, before it, among the unaware,"*

and Surah, 4:163-164,

> *"Indeed, we have revealed to you, [O Muhammad], as we revealed to Nooh (Noah) and the prophets after him. And we revealed to Ibrahim (Abraham), Ismaeel (Ishmael), Is-haaq (Isaac), Ya'qoub (Jacob), the descendants, Issa (Jesus), Ayyub(Job), Yunus (Jonah), Haroon (Aaron), and Suleyman (Solomon), and to Dawood (David) we gave the book [of (Zaboor) Psalms]. And sent messengers about whom we have related their stories to you before and messengers about whom we did not...."*

Here is a limited sampling of Qur'anic versions of Biblical events which have been "corrected" to support Islamic doctrines thus becoming at variance with the Bible:

---

24 The following Islamic links would provide ample documentation on this issue: http://www.inter-islam.org/Biographies/Hazisa39.html

http://www.searchtruth.com/book_display.php?book=030&translator=2&start=0&number=5837

http://en.rafed.net/islamic-articles-v15-1030/beliefs/12921-hadith-of-satan-s-defaming-all-sons-of-adam-except-jesus-and-mother

(a) Denial of the crucifixion of Issa (Jesus). The Qur'an vehemently attacks the very idea of the crucifixion of Issa as per Surah 4:157, "*And because of their saying, 'We killed Messiah Issa (Jesus), son of Maryam (Mary), the messenger of Allah,' - but they killed him not, nor crucified him, but it was made to appear to them to be so…*"

(b) The birth of Issa (Jesus) under a palm tree and not in a manger, as reported in the Bible. Surah 19:23 provides the text, "*And the pains of childbirth drove her to the trunk of a date-palm. She said: 'Would that I had died before this, and had been forgotten and out of sight!'*"

(c) Maryam (Mary) mother of Issa (Jesus) lived in the "Mihrab[25]"under the care of Zakariya (Zechariah) with no mention of Joseph, her legal husband. Surah 3:37 states, "*So her Lord (Allah) accepted her with goodly acceptance. He made her grow in a good manner and put her under the care of Zakariya. Every time he entered Al-Mihrab, he found her supplied with sustenance. He said: 'O Maryam, from where have you got this?' She said, 'This is from Allah.' Allah provides sustenance to whom he wills, without limit.'*"

(d) The Islamic Feast of Sacrifice (Eid Al-Adha) celebrated annually and integrated with pilgrimage rites, gives the impression that Islam proclaims some form of redemption/atonement. However, this is not the case at all. In point of fact, the concepts of redemption, and atonement through substitutional blood sacrifice are both anathemas and thus are anti-Islamic according to Surah's 6:164, 17:15,53:38, "*…no bearer of burdens can bear the burden of another…*". Zabeh (slaughter) in the specific sense of "sacrifice" occurs only once in the Qur'an in Surah 37:107, and then in regard to Ibrahim's "sacrifice" of Ismaeel. The notion of this usage is strict obedience to Allah, and has no redemptive implications whatsoever. Though the Qur'an doesn't mention Ismaeel (Ishmael) by name, it is a universally held belief by

---

25 The "Mihrab" A niche in the wall of a mosque that indicates the direction of Mecca where the prayer leader stands to lead the Muslim prayer. Thus the Qur'an is using this term to what a Christian or Jewish reader would assume to be the inner chamber of the Temple, where the priest carries out his duties. Note that there is a total absence in the Qur'an of naming the Jewish and Christian places of worship despite their widespread presence in the Arabia of Muhammad, and instead renaming them with Islamic terminology (such as Mihrab's, Masjid's), with one exception in Surah 22:40 where these are given obscure Arabic terms.

Muslims that it was Ismaeel that Ibrahim (Muslim name of Abraham) offered up when tested by Allah.[26]

(e) Ibrahim and his son Ismaeel rebuilding the central shrine in Mecca, the Kaaba![27] Surah 2:127 states, *"And when Ibrahim (Abraham) and Ismaeel (Ishmael) were raising the foundations of the house (i.e. the Kaaba) ...'"*

(f) The rites of the Hajj (Pilgrimage to Mecca as the fifth pillar [obligation] of Islam) established by Ibrahim, as per Surah 3:96-97, *"⁹⁶The first house (i.e. the Kaaba) appointed for mankind was that at Bakkah (Mecca), full of blessing, and a guidance for all creation (Angels, Jinns and mankind)⁹⁷...and Hajj (pilgrimage to Mecca) to the House (Kaaba) is a duty that mankind owes to Allah..."*

The above points are examples of a re-directed and re-cast Biblical time frame and narrative which starts out with a different definition of "God", and proceeds to support this new direction by altering each event, and character and doctrine to point to a new and completely different outcome.

3. Corruption through Making False Claims about Allah and his Prophets

As a continuation of the previous corruption charges through "falsification of events and doctrines", the Qur'an presents doctrinal counter arguments to the known Biblical doctrines as explicit "denials", but in the form of "corrections".

Typically a Muslim would ask, "How can God become a man? How can Allah have a son? How is three equal to one? How come the Bible shows that the prophets make so many blunders and sins: e.g. Did Lot really sleep with his daughters? How is it possible for Noah to get drunk? Did Abraham lie to Pharaoh?"

Here are some Qur'anic illustrations about this charge:

(a) Allah is NOT knowable: Surah 42:11 declares, *"...there is nothing whatever like unto Him ..."*

---

26 See fatwa: //http://islamqa.info/en/552
27 According to Islamic sources, the original Kaaba was built by Adam. http://www.al-islam.org/story-of-the-holy-kaaba-and-its-people-shabbar/kaaba-house-allah

(b) Allah is NOT a trinity: Surah 5:73, "*They have disbelieved (blasphemed) who say, 'Allah is the third of three.' And there is no god except one God. If they do not desist not from their blasphemy, a grievous penalty will befall them.*"

(c) Allah NEVER reveals himself: Surah 42:52, "*It is not given to any human being that Allah should speak to him unless by inspiration, or from behind a veil, or that he sends a messenger to reveal what he wills by his leave...*"

(d) Issa is NOT Lord (God incarnate): Surah 5:72, "*They have certainly blasphemed who say, 'Allah is the Messiah, the son of Maryam' while the Messiah has said, 'O Children of Israel, worship Allah , my Lord and your Lord.' Indeed, **he who associates others with Allah** - Allah has forbidden him paradise, and his refuge is the fire...*"

(e) Issa is NOT the Son of God:

    a. Surah 2:116, "*And they say: Allah has begotten a son. Glory be to him. To him belongs all that is in the heavens and on earth, and all surrender with obedience to him.*"

    b. Surah 5:17, "*Surely, in disbelief are they who say that Allah is the Messiah, son of Maryam (Mary). Say (O Muhammad): 'Who then has the least power against Allah, if he were to destroy the Messiah, son of Maryam (Mary), his mother, and all those who are on the earth together?' And to Allah belongs the dominion of the heavens and the earth, and all that is between them. He creates what he wills. And Allah is able to do all things.*"

    c. Surah 9:30, "*... the Christians say: Messiah is the son of Allah. That is a saying from their mouths. They imitate the saying of the disbelievers of old. Allah's curse be on them, how they are deluded away from the truth...*"

    d. Surah 4:172, "*Never would the Messiah disdain to be a slave of Allah, nor would the angels near to him. And whoever disdains his worship and is arrogant - He will gather them to himself all together.*"

Other counter arguments according to the Qur'an are:

(f) Misrepresentations of the Biblical account of the Triune God:

    a. Surah 72:3, "*And exalted be the majesty of our Lord, he has taken neither a wife, nor a son*"

    b. Surah 4:171, "*O People of the Scripture, do not commit excesses in your religion or say about Allah except the truth. The Messiah, Issa, the son of Maryam, was but a messenger of Allah and his word, which he conveyed unto Maryam, and a spirit from him. So believe in Allah and his messengers. And do not say, "three", desist, it is better for you. Indeed, Allah is but one god. Exalted is he above having a son...*"

    c. Surah, 5:116, "*And recall when Allah will say on the day of resurrection: 'O Issa (Jesus), son of Maryam (Mary): Did you say to the people, 'Worship me and my mother as two gods besides Allah?'*""

In the foregoing, having demonstrated the alleged false claims which were said to have been made by Jews and Christians about Allah; now we turn our attention to show how Muhammad himself is injected into the Biblical framework through the correction and recasting of the Biblical prophets, presenting them as Muslims and their mission to be Islam. Hence, the logical implication being that the Biblical narrative of these prophets pointing to Christ is a fabrication, and thus fraudulent. Therefore, forging a airtight charge of corruption.

(g) Instead of Biblical covenants and prophets pointing to Christ, Islam claims that all "prophets" point to Muhammad through the "Covenant of the Prophets":

    a. Surah 3:81, "*And when **Allah imposed a covenant**[28]**on the prophets:** Certainly what I have given you of the book and wisdom; then a messenger (i.e. Muhammad) comes to you verifying that which is with you, you must believe in him, and you must aid him. Allah said: Do you affirm and accept my covenant in this? They said: We do affirm. He said: Then bear witness, and I am with you among the witnesses.*'"

---

[28] This is not a covenant in the Biblical sense, but the term "covenant" is used here with a different definition. This is an imposed one-way "covenant" that infers no accountability on the part of Allah.

b. Surah 33:7, "*And when **we took from the prophets their covenant,** and from you (O Muhammad), and from Nooh (Noah), Ibrahim (Abraham), Moosa (Moses), and Issa (Jesus), son of Maryam (Mary). We took from them a strong covenant.*"

(h) Muhammad was the first Muslim even before Adam:

a. Surah 39:12, "*And I have been commanded to be the **first of the Muslims***"

b. Surah 6:14, "*…I am commanded to be the **first who declared his Islam**…*"

(i) Muhammad was the final messenger and "Seal of the Prophets": Surah 33:40, "*Muhammad is not the father of any man among you, but he is the messenger of Allah and the **Seal of the Prophets**…*"

(j) All "prophets and messengers" were Muslims:

a. Surah 2:136, "*Say (O Muslims), 'We believe in Allah and that which has been sent down to us and that which has been sent down to Ibrahim (Abraham), Ismaeel (Ishmael), Is-haq (Isaac), Ya'qub (Jacob), and to the Tribes, and that which has been given to Moosa (Moses) and Issa (Jesus), and that which has been given to the prophets from their Lord. we make no distinction between any of them, **and to him (Allah) we are Muslims**'*"

b. Surah 3:84, "*Say (O Muhammad): 'We believe in Allah and in what has been sent down to us, and what was sent down to Ibrahim (Abraham), Ismaeel (Ishmael), Is-haq (Isaac), Ya'qub (Jacob), the Tribes and what was given to Moosa (Moses), Issa (Jesus) and the prophets from their Lord. We make no distinction between one another among them **and to him (Allah) we are Muslims**.'*"

4. Corruption by Rewriting Own Book and Claiming or Attributing its Authorship to Allah

The following is a further illustration whereby there is a direct charge of corrupting the original text that came from the Eternal Tablet.

Typically a Muslim would ask, "You have so many different versions and translations of the Bible, which one can we trust?"

Here are some illustrations from the Qur'an regarding this charge:

(a) Surah 2:79 *"Then woe to those who write the Book with their own hands and then say, 'This is from Allah,' to purchase with it a little price. Woe to them for what their hands have written and woe to them for that they earn thereby."*

(b) Surah 2:75-78, "*75. Do you covet that they would believe you while a party of them used to hear the words of Allah and then distort them knowingly? 76. And when they meet the believers, they say, 'We believed'; but when they are alone with one another, they say, 'Do you talk to them about what Allah has revealed to you so they can argue with you about it before your Lord?' Then will you not reason? 77. But do they not know that Allah knows what they conceal and what they proclaim? 78. And among them are unlettered ones who do not know the Scripture except in wishful thinking, and they but guess."*

5. Corruption through Distortion of the Book and of Twisting of the Tongue

Having sidestepped the unanimous position of Muslim scholars regarding this charge, many Christian theologians and missiologists have opined that the distortion based on the "the twisting of the tongues", was:

a) Only verbal

b) Limited to the time period of Muhammad's life

c) Only an oral exercise that had no impact on the text itself.

Hence they claim that the Qur'anic view of Judeo-Christian scriptures is that they are intact and this charge does not stand.

However, the Muslim scholars' position is clear as evidenced in the discussion below and of course supported by authoritative Fatwa's[29].

This charge is given in three Surah's 5:13; 3:78; and 4:46. We will examine each separately and relate it to the four initial charges, as per the opinions expressed by the Muslim scholars themselves:

---

[29] Here are two important Fatwa's which would confirm our assertion: http://islamqa.info/en/2001 and http://islamqa.info/en/209007

> Surah 5:13 *"So for their breaking of the covenant we cursed them and made their hearts hard. **They distort words from their usages and have forgotten a portion of that of which they were reminded.** And you will still observe deceit among them, except a few. ..."*

This quotation reflects the following accusations:

a) Breaking of the covenant (See for example, Surah 3:81 regarding the covenant of the prophets)

b) Distorting words (Implies redefinition of actual text)

c) Forgetting or ignoring a portion (Implies textual omission)

d) Deceit and forgery (In rewriting, redefining, and replacing)

The above four items (a-d) are summary of the initial four charges, that is to say: corruption by omission and concealment (a and d above), by falsifying events and doctrines (c and d above), making false claims about Allah and his prophets (a, b, c, and d above), and rewriting their own scriptures (c and d above).

As for the phrase *"except a few of them"* the unanimous Islamic commentary is that is passage refers to those Jews and Christians who embraced Islam and thus were **not** considered deceitful.

> Surah 3:78, *"And indeed, there is among them a party who alter the Scripture with their tongues so you may think it is from the Scripture, but it is not from the Scripture. And they say, 'This is from Allah,' but it is not from Allah. And they speak untruth about Allah while they know."*

This quotation reflects the following accusations:

a) Altering the scripture with their tongues,

b) Saying, "this is from Allah", and

c) Speaking untruth about Allah knowingly.

Although this gives the appearance of referring only to the "verbal" redefinitions and omissions as discussed earlier, it must be taken within the full context of Qur'anic references to Biblical corruption as documented in Charges 1-4 above. Instead, most Christian scholars have chosen to put the focus literally on "the altering of the scriptures with their own tongues", and thus out of context.

Another aspect of the full context that is being ignored by some Christian scholars is the language in which the Jews and Christians of Muhammad's day were reciting these "altered scriptures." However the assumption by Muslim scholars is that these recitations were in Arabic, so it would follow that the Jews and Christians were knowingly tampering with the written text as well as their oral recitation.

This is then illustrated in:

> Surah 4:46, "*Among those who are Jews, there are some who displace words from (their) right places and say: 'We hear your word (O Muhammad) and disobey,' and 'Hear and let you (O Muhammad) hear nothing.' And ra'ina with a twist of their tongues and as a mockery of the religion (Islam).* And if only they had said: 'We hear and obey', and 'Do make us understand,' it would have been better for them, and more proper, but Allah has cursed them for their disbelief, so they believe not except a few."

This reflects the following accusations:

a) Displacing words from their right places, (Infers textual change, i.e. Tahreef)

b) Hearing and disobeying

c) Making mockery of the religion "with the twist of their tongues"

d) Disbelief.

Hence, Allah has cursed them. So it can be seen that the twisting of the tongue charge had as much to do with charges of the Jews play on words—whereby they pretended to honor and respect Muhammad, while covertly ridiculing him—as it does to the process of verbal obfuscation which would impact the text.

Further Affirmations of Biblical Corruption by Inference

The above are the most egregious five charges of Biblical corruption, but the Qur'an abounds in less obvious inferences in support of these, as per the following Surah's:

- Surah 3:19, "*The religion before Allah is Islam: Nor did the People of the Book dissent therefrom except through envy of each other, after knowledge had come to them. But if any deny the signs of Allah, Allah is swift in calling to account.*"

- Surah 3:85, "*If anyone desires a religion other than Islam, never will it be accepted of him; and in the hereafter he will be in the ranks of the losers.*"

- Surah 33:7, "*And remember we took from the prophets their covenant: As (we did) from you (Muhammad): from Nooh, Ibrahim, Moosa, and Issa the son of Maryam: We took from them a solemn covenant.*"

- Surah 3:81, "*Behold! Allah took the covenant of the prophets, saying: 'I give you a book and wisdom; then comes to you an apostle (i.e. Muhammad), confirming what is with you; do ye believe in him and render him help.' Allah said: 'Do you agree, and take this my covenant as binding on you?' They said: 'We agree.' He said: 'Then bear witness, and I am with you among the witnesses.'*"

- Surah 10:94, "*So, if you (Muhammad) are in doubt concerning what we have revealed to you, then question those who read the scripture before you. The truth from your Lord has come to you; so do not be of the ones who waver.*"

- Surah 9:33, "*He it is who has sent his messenger with the guidance and the religion of truth, that he may manifest it over every religion, even though the disbelievers be averse.*"

- Surah 48:28, "*It is he who has sent his messenger with guidance and the religion of truth, that he may make it prevail over all religion. And Allah suffices as witness.*"

- Surah 48:29, "*Muhammad is the messenger of Allah and those who are with him are ruthless against the disbelievers, merciful among themselves. You see them bowing and prostrating. They seek bounty from Allah. Their mark on their foreheads is from the effect of prostration. That is their description in the Tawrat and in the Injeel...*"

- Surah 3:110, "*You are the best community (i.e. Ummah) brought forth to all humans, enjoining Islamic monotheism (Tawheed), and forbidding blasphemy (Kufr), and believing in Allah. Had the People of the Scripture believed, it would have been better for them; some of them are believers; but most of them are wicked.*"

Verdict of Corruption Charges

"Sameness" relates to the foundational Islamic claim and supporting narrative that all previous scriptures were nothing but earlier and limited "editions" of the Qur'an with its central doctrine of "Tawheed" (Islamic Monotheism), thus countering every single doctrine of Biblical Christianity, and by implication necessitating the charge of Biblical corruption.

This "sameness" claim has served Islam on two fronts:

(a) It provided the rationale for linking Islam to the Biblical narrative as being the "same," while simultaneously claiming corruption and thus the need for "correction".

(b) It then accomplished this "correction" of the Biblical revelation through the construction of a counter narrative, claiming it to be the true original that is consistent with Islamic monotheism (Tawheed) as well as the line of prophecies predicting the coming of Muhammad as the seal of all the prophets, with the final corrected message for all creation and for all time.

We amply demonstrated from the pages of the Qur'an and the disciplines of interpretation by Muslim scholars that the "sameness" Islamic claims and assertions are clear statements to declare that all previous scriptures that "came down" to the prophets and messengers, such as the Tawrat, the Zaboor, and the Injeel, were nothing more than limited earlier editions of the Qur'an as they all emanated from the Eternal Tablet, the Mother of the Book.

Even those Qur'anic Ayah's that on their face value gave credence to the Tawrat, Zaboor, and the Injeel, were seen as clear affirmations of the Muslimhood of the previous prophets (like Abraham, Moses and Jesus). Furthermore, not only does the Qur'an claim Biblical corruption, but that this corruption is affirmed in so many ways. Our attempt to group the corruption charges into five categories is but a limited effort in providing an initial understanding of the many other claims inherent in this central Islamic doctrine of Biblical corruption.

Thus, we state that this "sameness" claim is nothing but a veiled ploy that served to build the legitimacy of Muhammad's mission (i.e. prophethood) while at the same time, countering and denying the foundational Biblical narrative and the provable historical timeline, affecting each and every Biblical doctrine.

Chapter 3

The "Process" of Qur'anic "Revelation"

Components of the Process

Since every Muslim without exception believes that Allah is the direct author of the Qur'an—regardless of sect, levels of piety, education, or any other consideration—it is important to understand the process of how this "revelation" was delivered to "mankind" through Muhammad.

Having introduced the "same and not the same" theme as well as the resultant corruption charges, we turn our attention as to how these themes play out in the form and method of Qur'anic "revelation". For if the Allah of Islam were to be the same as the LORD God of the Judeo-Christian scriptures the concept and the format of his revelations would at least be more than "sufficiently similar" if not precisely the same. But in fact, far from being an issue of direct correspondence, there is no resemblance whatsoever, as to the process, or the end result.

In order to comprehend the total lack of resemblance on the one hand, and the high level of foundational differences on the other, we need to consider *how* the Islamic source—the Eternal Tablet, i.e. "Mother of the Book"—emerged on the scene through Muhammad, and then *how* this event led to the final Qur'an. According to Islamic documentation this involved a four-pronged and intertwined process, composed of:

1. The "Wahy" (i.e. Islamic Inspiration),

2. "Tanzil" (i.e. Coming Down),

3. "Jibril" (i.e. Agent of communication), and

4. "Asbab Annuzul" (i.e. The reasons for coming down).

Generally speaking, Qur'anic "revelation" is a complex process occurring in stages, but culminating in the ultimate delivery of Allah's final book, the Qur'an, to Muhammad.

At first it involved the initial "coming down" of the entire "Eternal Tablet" that has inscribed on it all of the divine information, or text needed by mankind, from the highest heaven (i.e. 7th heaven) to the lowest heaven (i.e. 1st heaven) near to the Earth. According to Islamic sources, this would have included all of the previous Judeo-Christian revelations.

This alleged "coming down" of the "Eternal Tablet" is said to have happened during the month of Ramadan at the beginning of Muhammad's mission in 610 A.D.

> Surah 2:185, "*The month of Ramadan is that in which the Qur'an came down, a guidance for the all mankind and clear proofs of guidance and criterion....*"

Once the Eternal Tablet made it to the nearest heaven to earth, Muhammad needed to continue to receive information from it. The subsequent transmission of this information was said to have been communicated through angel Jibril (i.e. the Islamic version of "Gabriel") directly to Muhammad's heart, as in Surah 2:97:

> "*Say, 'Whoever is an enemy to Jibril - it is none but he who has **brought the Qur'an down upon your heart,** [O Muhammad], by permission of Allah, confirming that which was before it** and as guidance and good tidings for the believers,'*"

This step of transmission to Muhammad's "heart" is termed "inspiration" (Wahy), whereby Muhammad would in turn repeat Jibril's inspired words, or dictate them out loud to his human record keepers bit by bit. This piecemeal process was accomplished mostly through inquiry as specific situations arose during his proclamations from 610 A.D. up until his death in 632 A.D.

In what follows we provide basic descriptions of each component of this process—primarily to demonstrate indelibly how distant and distinct this entire process is from the revelation of the Biblical scriptures.

1. The "Wahy" (Islamic Inspiration)

Wahy is an Arabic term meaning, "inspiration." All supernatural communication between Allah and his messengers is said to be through angelic beings who in turn communicate with the prophets and messengers of Allah.

The Islamic concept of "inspiration" is shrouded in secrecy. However, the Qur'an declares three forms of Wahy as per Surah 42:51:

1) By Inspiration,

2) From behind a veil, or

3) Through an angelic messenger.

In sharp contrast to the LORD God of the Bible, Allah never speaks directly to any man, as we see in:

> *"It is not fitting for a man that Allah should speak to him except by **inspiration**, or from **behind a veil**, or by the **sending of a messenger** to reveal, with Allah's permission, what Allah wills: for he is most high, most wise."* (Surah 42:51)

Every messenger/prophet like Ibrahim, Moosa, or Issa received Wahy limited to their people and their time,

> *"We did send apostles before thee and appointed for them wives and children: and it was never the part of an apostle to bring a Sign except as Allah permitted (or commanded). **For each period is a Book**,"*(Surah 13:38)

while Muhammad had a final and superior status,

> *"2. ...Your companion (Muhammad) has neither gone astray nor has erred. 3. Nor does he speak of (his own) desire. 4. It is only an inspiration that is inspired. 5. He has been taught by one mighty in power,"* (Surah 53:2-5)

a status that is intended for all mankind, as well as for the Jinn, and for all eternity:

> • Surah 21:107, *"And we have sent you (O Muhammad) not but as a mercy for the worlds (all creation composed of angelic beings, Jinn, humans, and satanic beings)."*

- Surah 68:52, *"But it is nothing less than a message to all the worlds."*

- Surah 81:27, *"This is no less than a message to all the worlds."*

So we have established that Muhammad's "message" is for all creation and for all time. However, his message is not only composed of "inspired words", but also his "person"—meaning that all of his actions, and behaviors are also "Wahy."

Severe Implications: Muhammad's Very "Actions" Are Considered to be "Revelation"

What does that mean? Not just his "words" are considered "Wahy", but his actions are considered Wahy, as well, and therefore authoritative—meaning the way he walks, the way he eats, the way he trims his beard, the positions he takes for prayer—everything.

- Surah 68:4, *"And you (Muhammad) are an exalted standard of character."*

- Surah 33:21, *"Ye have indeed in the apostle of Allah (Muhammad) a beautiful pattern of conduct for anyone whose hope is in Allah and the final day and who engages much in the praise of Allah."*

As one can easily deduce, this elevation of all of Muhammad's words, deeds, and actions as a "model" of behavior is close to embodiment, and clearly sets the rationale as to the importance of Muhammad's "Sunnah" as the second most important of the Islamic sources for Islamic Jurisprudence.

A further implication is that the Qur'an cannot be implemented without the Sunnah as referenced by the Surah's above and others, as the prayer rituals are contained in the Sunnah not the Qur'an. And this is just one simple and key example to illustrate the implications as elaborated upon in Chapter 4.

2. Tanzil (Coming Down)

Tanzil literally means, "coming down." It is derived from the Arabic root word "Nazala—To come down." The notion of Tanzil emerges from the belief that the Qur'an itself is embodied physically in the Eternal Tablet (i.e. the "Mother of the Book") and is normally situated up above in the highest heavens, while mankind and Jinn are said to inhabit the earth. Therefore, in between the earth and heavens there are 7 heavens and 7 earths.

Surah 65:12, "*Allah is he who **created seven firmaments and of the earth a similar number**. Through the midst of them (all) **descends his command:** that you may know that Allah has power over all things, and that Allah comprehends all things...*"

So the Tanzil refers to the physical action of the Tablet—containing all previous and current editions of the Qur'an, including what the Qur'an refers to as the "Tawrat, Zaboor, and Injeel"—having literally "come down" through the 7 layers of the heavens to hover near the earth in the lowest level of the outer atmospheric realm.

It is from this nearby vantage point that it was "communicated" piecemeal (case by case) to Muhammad through the courier services of the angel Jibril.

Basically the process of the Tanzil as described above has been claimed to have been the same throughout history, including all the previous 103 books discussed earlier, that came down from the Eternal Tablet to earlier prophets and messengers—from Adam to Issa—prior to the 7th century when the "corrected version "and final installment of the Qur'an came down to Muhammad.

Surah 3:3, "*He has **sent down** upon you, [O Muhammad], the Book in truth**, confirming what was before it. And he brought down the Tawrat and the Injeel**.*"

Note that it is not only the process of the "coming down" that is being claimed as being the "same", it is the textual content of the Tawrat, Zaboor and the Injeel as well that are held to be confirming the Qur'an.

3. Jibril: The Agent/Medium of the Coming Down

The Qur'an declares that the angelic agent of this coming down and the inspiration (Tanzil and Wahy) is Jibril, who Muslim scholars associate with the Angel Gabriel, as mentioned earlier, and as referenced in Surah 2:97-98,

"***97.** Say (O Muhammad): 'Whoever is an enemy to **Jibril** (Gabriel)**, for indeed he has brought it (this Qur'an) down to your heart** by Allah's permission, confirming what came before it [i.e. the Tawrat (Torah) and the Injeel (Gospel)] and guidance and glad tidings for the believers. **98.** 'Whoever is an enemy to*

Allah, his angels, his messengers, Jibril (Gabriel) and Mikael (Michael), then Allah is an enemy to the disbelievers (i.e. non-Muslims).'"

Jibril is universally agreed upon by Islamic scholars, as well as ordinary Muslims, as the same being as the Archangel Gabriel of the Biblical scriptures, although Jibril is constitutionally different, in every way—as we shall demonstrate.

Now this Jibril is also referred to as Ruh-Al-Qudus (literally, holy spirit, not to be confused with the Biblical understanding of the Holy Spirit, the third person of the Triune God) according to Surah 16:102.

> *"Say (O Muhammad) **Ruh-ul-Qudus** (literally, holy spirit) **has brought it down(the Qur'an)** from your Lord with truth, that it may make firm and strengthen those who believe (Muslims) and as a guidance and glad tidings to those who have submitted (to Allah as Muslims)."*

In Surah 26:192-193, Jibril is referred to as Ruh Al-Amin (trustworthy spirit),

> *"¹⁹²·And truly, this (the Qur'an) is a revelation from the Lord of the worlds (mankind, Jinns and all that exists), ¹⁹³·which the **Ruh-Al Amin** [Jibril] has brought down."*

To add to the complexity of the situation, although the word, "Ruh" corresponds to the word "spirit", we are reminded in Surah 17:85 that Muhammad's understanding of the "spirit" is limited,

> Surah 17:85, *"And they ask you (O Muhammad) concerning the **Ruh (the Spirit)**; Say: 'The Ruh (the Spirit): it is one of the things, the knowledge of which is only with my Lord. And of knowledge (regarding the spirit), you have been given only a little.'"*

Who is this Jibril? Is he the same as the angel Gabriel we find in the Biblical scriptures?

Could he be the one who appeared to the Prophet Daniel (who is not mentioned in the Qur'an, by the way), or to the Virgin Mary? Or is he some other being?

This aspect is critical in our exposure of the issues, since the nature of "revelation" in Islam and therefore the identity of Jibril are inextricably intertwined.

As a test, hypothetically—would the Gabriel of the Bible really say *any* of these?

a. Surah 2:97, "*Say (O Muhammad): 'Whoever is an enemy to Jibril, for indeed he has brought this Qur'an down to your heart by Allah's permission, confirming what came before it and guidance and glad tidings for the believers.*"

b. Surah 2:98, "*Whoever is an enemy to Allah, his Angels, his messengers, Jibril and Mikael, then Allah is an enemy to the disbelievers.*"

c. Surah 66:4, "*If you two (Muhammad's wives) repent to Allah, yet your hearts certainly inclined; but if you support one another against him, Allah is his protector, and Jibril, and the righteous among the believers; and, after that, the angels are his supporters.*"

d. Surah 19:17, "*She (Maryam) placed a screen to screen herself from them; then we sent to her our spirit [angel Jibril], and he appeared before her in the form of a man in all respects.*"

And most especially the following Surah makes claims about Issa being taught by Jibril while in the cradle to defend his mother against charges of moral impropriety as well as other outrageous claims:

e. Surah 19:27-31, "*Then, carrying him, she brought him to her folk and they said, 'O Maryam, truly you have done a curious thing! O sister of Aaron your father was not a wicked man, nor was your mother unchaste'. Thereat she pointed to him. They said, 'How can we talk to one who is in the cradle?' He said, 'Lo, I am Allah's servant. He has given me the scripture and made me a prophet. And he has made me blessed wherever I may be and he has enjoined upon me prayer and alms giving, as long as I remain alive; and he made me dutiful towards my mother. And he has not made me arrogant, wretched. And peace be upon me the day I was born, and the day I die, and the day I shall be raised alive!*"

a. Surah 5:110, "*(Remember) when Allah will say (on the Day of Resurrection). 'O Issa (Jesus), son of Maryam (Mary), remember my favor to you and to your mother when I supported you with Ruh-ul-Qudus [Jibril] so that you spoke to the people in the cradle and in maturity; and when I taught you writing, wisdom, the Tawrat (Torah) and the Injeel (Gospel); and when you made*" *out of the clay, as it were, the figure of a bird, by my permission, and you breathed into it, and it became a bird by my permission, and you healed those born blind, and the lepers by my permission, and when you brought forth the dead by my permission; and when I restrained the children of Israel from you, since you came unto them with clear proofs, and the disbelievers among them said: 'This is nothing but evident magic.'"*

But most outrageously, the Biblical Gabriel would never deny the crucifixion of Jesus:

b.   Surah 4:157, "*That they said, 'We killed Christ Issa the son of Maryam the Apostle of Allah'; but they killed him not nor crucified him but so it was made to appear to them and those who differ therein are full of doubts with no knowledge, but only conjecture to follow, for of a surety they killed him not.*"

In short, as this hypothetical line of questionings attest, the Islamic Jibril is far from being the same as the Biblical Archangel Gabriel. So we can rest assured that the Jibril of the Qur'an is a completely different being, with a completely different message.[30]

4. Asbab Annuzul: The Reasons for the "Coming Down"

Every time Muhammad was faced with a situation or event to comment on and resolve, he had to "ask" and then "wait" to receive the "revelation" that would "come down" via the "Wahy."

Hence, the entire discipline of "Asbab Annuzul", which translates to "The Reasons for Coming Down".

The prerequisite regarding the "reasons for the coming down", is used heavily by Muslim scholars and expositors to provide the background events associated with the issue at hand in order to facilitate current and future decisions for guidance or judgment. The overwhelming majority of the Qur'anic text "came down" in bits and pieces based on the particular issue at hand.

---

30 For further examples of what Gabriel would never say, see Chapter 2, subsection entitled, "2. Corruption through Falsification of Events and Doctrines"

A familiar term that might capture those instances whereby Muhammad received "Wahy" in response to events or questions arising from within his Muslim community or challenges presented to him by non-Muslims might best be illustrated by the Western judicial term "case by case basis". However, this does not mean that all of the "revelation" was in response to such current events of the time.

However, one could then say that this process of inquiry produced a type of "situational ethics" through the establishment of a framework of prescribed and mandated answers to all the questions of mankind under the guise of being the revelation of "Allah's will".

As we shall see, there is no set of absolutes, but instead the completed Qur'an provides at best a situational "guidance" or "straight path" based on rules, mandates, and prescribed actions, combined with the separate but integral model of Muhammad's application of such "guidance" that he was to be emulated during his lifetime and forever by Muslims. This explains why the Qur'an *cannot* be applied without constant reference to the Sunnah of Muhammad.

Chapter 4

The Islamic Counter Narrative

Central Claims of Islam

This Islamic counter-narrative as expressed in the pages of the Qur'an is based on a set of connected claims, which fully counter the Biblical "Crimson Thread"—the thread that all scripture pointed to Christ. Here is a brief summary of those connected Islamic claims:

1. The claim that the "true religion", i.e. Islam, requires the belief in the one Allah and with Muhammad as his prophet and messenger as expressed in the Islamic creed, the Shahadah.

2. The claim that this belief represented the true original monotheism that was expressed in the original books that came down to the Biblical prophets and messengers.

3. The claim that all the prophets and messengers were sent by Allah to preach Islam and to acknowledge the coming of Muhammad.

4. The claim that Jews and Christians have corrupted their scriptures primarily by removing reference to Muhammad, and then by changing the text of the Bible to fit such removal.

Based on these claims, the Qur'an proceeds to reconstruct the lives and messages of the Biblical characters to develop key Islamic doctrines, while opposing the original Biblical ones. The readers of the Qur'anic versions of these stories may be taken aback, first by the apparent similarities in names, and then by the stark contrast of the details.

Before we delve into the details of these stories, we start by a recap of the original message of Islamic monotheism as expressed in the Islamic creed, the Shahadah.

The Shahadah Sets the Stage

The Shahadah,[31] the Islamic creed, states: *No deity but Allah and Muhammad is the messenger of Allah.*

This assertion merged the call to return to "Islamic Monotheism", with a clear elevation of Muhammad. It is generally believed that this foundational claim evolved rather quickly into the full doctrine of the "Oneness of Allah" (i.e. Tawheed) declaring it to be the same as the original revelation given to all the preceding Judeo-Christian prophets, but which was allegedly "corrupted"—so that he (Muhammad) was sent to "correct, purify and consolidate" as the "Seal of all the Prophets."

Furthermore, as the Qur'anic revelations emerged in bits and pieces there was no reference as to how one could or should worship Allah, leaving the details to be explained by Muhammad through what he said, did or consented to, i.e. Muhammad's Sunnah (example/pattern). In other words, through the institution of the Shahadah, Muhammad established himself as the sole arbiter of who Allah is and how to worship/serve him—not only during his lifetime but for all times. For in it and through it the "confessing Muslim" must renounce and denounce all other beliefs and pay sole allegiance to both Allah and Muhammad.[32]

Redefining of the Biblical Stories

Having declared himself to be the final authority without proof of any kind, Muhammad claimed prophetic lineage back to the known prophets to substantiate his claims by producing different versions of their stories and incorporating them into the Qur'an to "correct" and redirect the narrative to support Islamic doctrines. Of course, all of these characters were Muslims by definition:

---

31 Although the "Shahadah" is not stated explicitly in the Qur'an, its 2 components, Allah and Muhammad, are given in Surah references such as: 3:2, "*Allah - there is no deity except him, the ever-living, the sustainer of existence*"; 48:29, "*Muhammad is the messenger of Allah ...*"; 33:40, "*Muhammad is never the father of any one of your men, but is the messenger of Allah and the seal of the prophets...*". See also the following Islamic link on the tenets of Islam including the Shahadah: http://islamqa.info/en/13569
32 Of course this is fully documented and detailed in the "Doctrine of Allegiance and Rejection, Al-walaa' wal Baraa'". See, Sam Solomon and E. Al Maqdidi, The Common Word: The Undermining the Church. ANM Publishers, 2008.

- Surah 3:84, "*Say (O' Muhammad), 'We have believed in Allah and in what was revealed to us and what was revealed to Ibrahim, Ismael, Ishaq, Ya'qoob, and the tribes, and in what was given to Moosa and Issa and to the prophets from their Lord. We make no distinction between any of them, and we are all Muslims.'*"

- Surah 10:72, "*...and I (Nooh/Noah) have been commanded to be of the Muslims.*"

- Surah 3:67, "*Ibrahim (Islamic name given to Abraham) was neither a Jew nor a Christian, but he was a 'Hanafi' Muslim. And he was not of the polytheists.*"

- Surah 12:101, "*... Cause me (Yusuf/Joseph) to die a Muslim and join me with the righteous.*"

Islamic scholars would piece together these stories to create a graphical illustration called "Tree of the Prophets and Messengers" (see Figure 2) based on this evolution of the Qur'anic narrative.

Woven in the evolving textual entity that became the Qur'an, is the redefinition and rebuilding (i.e. "correction") of the Biblical characters to fit with the Qur'anic doctrine of Islamic Monotheism (Tawheed) as expressed in the Islamic creed, "*No god but Allah and Muhammad is the messenger of Allah.*"

The following sections explain in detail this recasting of the stories of key Biblical characters by examining the "Tree of the Prophets and Messengers". At the "root" of this tree—with the creation of the Muslim version of Adam—the central Christian doctrines of original sin, redemption, promise of a Savior and the fulfillment of this promise through Christ Jesus, are all countered by the Islamic doctrines of Fitrah, the Muslimhood of all mankind, the absence of original sin, the prophets/messengers proclaiming the coming of Muhammad, and the finality of Muhammad as the "Seal of the Prophets".

As one goes up this tree we encounter the so-called "Anchor Prophets." These are: Nooh (Islamized name of Noah), Ibrahim (Islamized name of Abraham), Moosa (Islamized name of Moses), Issa (Islamized name of Jesus) and finally of course, added as number five and final within the list—Muhammad.

By focusing on these select characters (other than Muhammad, whose role is to be discussed in more depth in Chapter 5), and their Islamized stories we gain an in-depth understanding of key Islamic doctrines, doctrines which counter the very foundations of Biblical Christianity.

Tree of the Prophets

The "Tree" Provides a "Corrective "Counter-Biblical Summary

Internally, this "tree" has been used by Islamic scholars and teachers to summarize graphically the Islamic historical narrative which starts with the creation of the Muslim Adam at the root, upwards through Idris (Enoch), Nooh (Noah) continuing up to Ibrahim (Abraham), where the tree branches to the left through the Is-haq (Isaac) branch, to continue through the Hebrew prophets and messengers culminating with the Muslim prophet Issa (Jesus). But the right branch progresses through Ismaeel (Ishmael) directly to Muhammad as the "light of the world".

The writings associated with this tree, as given by Islamic sources (Figure 2) provide the details of Islamic thinking and interpretations—all guided by the Qur'anic texts which would portray the full Muslimhood of all these characters, while showing Muhammad as the culmination of Allah's efforts to "guide" Jinn and mankind to Islam.

The Muslim Adam: Doctrinal Divergence at the Root of the "Tree"

Main Divergence: A Very Different "First Man"

The Islamic divergence from the Biblical narrative—or rather the intentional deconstruction of the Biblical narrative—starts with the Muslim version of "Adam" as depicted at the "root" of the "Tree of the Prophets." (Figure 2)

Islamic sources portray the Muslim Adam as the father figure of mankind, yet a very different one from the Biblical Adam. He was created differently, made only a "slip" when he ate from the forbidden tree, fell from paradise, but was fully pardoned, and was guided by Allah in Islam.

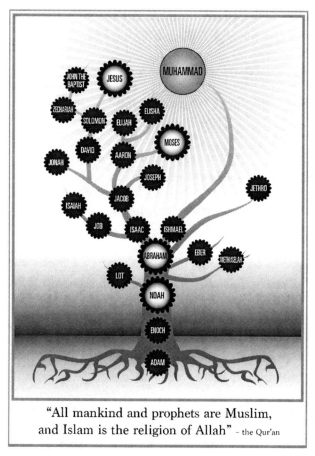

"All mankind and prophets are Muslim,
and Islam is the religion of Allah" – the Qur'an

Figure 2: Simplified Artist's rendering of the Islamic "Tree of the Prophets": Shows the Islamic identity and genealogy of the "prophets", starting with Adam, branching at Ibrahim (Abraham), with the Is-haq (Isaac) line ending with Prophet Issa (Jesus) and the Ismaeel (Ishmael) line ending with Muhammad.

How Was the Muslim Adam Created?

The Muslim Adam *was not* created in the "image" of the LORD God, *did not* have a personal relationship with the living LORD God in Eden, *did not* plunge all mankind into the state of "original sin" (as the consequence of his disobedience), and so *did NOT need* a savior to rescue him from sin and restore his relationship with his creator. Instead, he was created as a *mortal* in a "state of felicity" whereby he was already "submitted" to Allah, and was only in need of "guidance" (rules).

Furthermore, the Qur'an provides various alternatives on "how" the Muslim Adam was created, with descriptions that systematically avoid any trace of having been "created in Allah's image". The most operative Ayah on the complete absence on any form of "likeness" is given in,

Surah 42:11, "…*There is nothing like unto Him …*".

But, if not "in Allah's image", how was the Muslim Adam created? The following Surah's provide a series of possibilities:

- Surah 96:1-2, "*Proclaim (or read) in the name of thy Lord who created, **created man, out of a clot of congealed blood**…*"

- Surah 15:26, "*We **created man from sounding clay**, from mud molded into shape…*"

- Surah 23:12-14 "*Man we **did create from a quintessence (of clay)**; Then we placed him **as (a drop of) sperm in a place of rest**, firmly fixed; Then we made the sperm into a clot of congealed blood; then of that clot we made a lump; then we made out of that lump bones and clothed the bones with flesh; then we developed out of it another creature. So blessed be Allah, the best to create!*"

- Surah 25:54, "*It is he who has **created man from water.***"

- Surah 16:4, "*He has created man from a **sperm drop**…*"

Furthermore, rather than exhibiting the characteristics of being given "dominion" and the intellect to freely exercise such dominion, we discover that the Muslim Adam was created "weak", "forgetful" and naturally created into "toil and struggle":

- Surah 4:28, "*…. man was **created weak**.*"

- Surah 20:115, "*And we had already taken a promise from Adam before, but he **forgot**; and we found not in him determination.*"

- Surah 90:4, "*We have created man **into toil and struggle**,*"

These forms of creation all counter the central Biblical theme of creating man in the LORD God's image. The theme of "no image, no likeness" is carried throughout the Qur'an, whereby any trace or implications of likeness being seen as the ultimate "Shirk" or "blasphemy."

"Original Sin" vs. a "Slip"! The Qur'anic Version of the "Fall"?

According to the Islamic narrative when this Adam made a "mistake" or a "slip", he was immediately "repented upon, and forgiven" by Allah's fiat:

- Surah 2:36, "*Then Satan made them slip, and get them out of the state in which they had been. We said: 'All of you get down with enmity between yourselves. On earth will be your dwelling-place and your means of livelihood - for a time.'*"

- Surah 2:37, "*Then Adam received from his Lord words. And **his Lord repented on him**. He is the one who accepts repentance, the most merciful.*"

- Surah 2:38, "*We said: 'Get you down all from here; and if, as is sure, there comes to you guidance from me, whosoever follows my guidance, on them shall be no fear, nor shall they grieve.'*"

In another account, he simply "erred" i.e. made a "mistake":

- Surah 20:121, "*And Adam and his wife ate of it, and their private parts became apparent to them, and they began to fasten over themselves from the leaves of paradise. And Adam disobeyed his Lord and **erred**.*"

So that when he ate the fruit, he was exiled or thrown out of the Islamic paradise <u>down</u> to earth together with his wife and Satan. This is then the Islamic version of the "Fall".

Interestingly, Islamic traditions would state that Muslim Adam landed on Mount Arafah[33], near Mecca, whereas his "wife"[34] had landed in India and would join him after she had wandered for a long time! Later on Muslim Adam would build the Kaaba, which would be the central shrine of Islam.

Although the Qur'an does not explain why he was thrown out from the Islamic paradise down to earth, it would state that Muslim Adam was first pardoned upon landing on earth (Surah 2:37) and then he would enjoy life on earth for

---

33 This assumed "fact" was incorporated into the Hajj rites, whereby the starting rites consist of "standing on Mount Arafah" and reciting Surah 7:172 this committing all mankind to submit to Allah in Islam.

34 The Qur'an does not mention Adam's "wife" by name.

a while till he would die. So "death" was already a given (Surah 67:2, "*It is he (Allah) who has created death and life.*") and was not a result of the Islamic version of the "Fall".

In fact by claiming the building of the Kaaba by Adam, we are given a strong glimpse into the beginnings of Allah's "guidance" as stated in Surah 2:38 above. Of course, in the Qur'an, "guidance" means Islam.

The "Fitrah Doctrine": Denies Man's Sin Nature by Substituting Muslimhood of Mankind

Following up on the Islamic "creation" story whereby there was no "original sin", the Qur'an continues with an important twist, whereby Allah imposes a requirement on all mankind to accept him as the only god—i.e. all are born Muslims, i.e. submitted to Allah:

> Surah 7:172, "*When your Lord drew forth from the children of Adam - from their loins - their descendants, and made them testify concerning themselves: 'Am I not your Lord?'- They said: 'Yes, we do testify lest you should say on the day of judgment: Of this we were never mindful'*"

Thus, the Qur'an provides an explicit conclusion associated with this "imposed one-way covenant":

> Surah 30:30, "*So set you (O Muhammad) your face according to the pattern on which he has made mankind (Allah's Fitrah, i.e. creation of man submitted to him as Muslim), with which he has created mankind...*"

Summary about Muslim Prophet Adam (vs. the Biblical Adam):

- **Denied**: The Muslim Adam was not created in Allah's image, (The significance is that: Allah's nature cannot be known, as there is nothing like unto Allah, so to make mankind "in his image" would be an anathema and a blasphemy. This omission in the Islamic version of the Adamic story foreshadows further Qur'anic prohibitions against any form of "association" with Allah (sonship) or "humanization" of Allah (fatherhood), including the ultimate anathema of the "incarnation" of the LORD God in Christ Jesus.)

- **Omitted**:

  a. The Muslim Adam did not receive the Edenic Covenant: Allah only imposes covenants, like the Fitrah, the requirement that all mankind is submitted to him in Islam.

  b. Allah did not walk in the garden with the Muslim Adam: There was no intimate relationship, no direct revelation, no incarnation, and no need to restore the relationship through the sacrifice on the cross and no indwelling.

  c. The Muslim Adam did not suffer the permanent effect of the "Fall" when he disobeyed Allah. Instead, he was after all, weak, made a slip, hence was pardoned, and most importantly needed the guidance of Islam.

  d. The Biblically significant story of Cain and Abel is countered in the Qur'an without any reference to the great significance to the "Blood Sacrifice."

- **Added**:

  a. Muslim Adam—Allah imposed a new nature on mankind through a one-way "covenant" (mandate) called the Fitrah (the natural man is a Muslim). In effect this replaces and denies man's sin nature or original sin, thus replacing the need for salvation.

  b. Muslim Adam accepted imposed covenant from Allah to declare Muhammad as the seal of the prophets

  c. Muslim Adam was the recipient of the "coming down" of 10 books from the Eternal Tablet of the Qur'an.

Anchor Prophets: Nooh, Ibrahim, Moosa, Issa, Muhammad

These five prophets are known as the "Anchor Prophets" (Ulul-Azm, in Arabic) in the Qur'an. Although the Qur'an states that "*there is no distinction*" (Surah 2:136), among the prophets, as a group these five are more elevated than others, with Muhammad being at the highest level. Thus according to Surah 2:253, "*Those messengers some we have preferred above others …and some he raised in rank…*"

They each presumably started a new school or dispensation, with each given a "Shariah" (law) for their time, limited only to the people they were sent to, with the exception of Muhammad—who is said to have brought the final and eternal Shariah to all mankind and all creation (Angels, Jinn, mankind, nature).

Therefore, all previous Shariah's are now abrogated and replaced by the Islamic Shariah—hence Muhammad is the best of the Anchor Prophets, being the alleged "Seal of the Prophets".

In the following section, we provide further insight into the reconstructed stories of the Anchor Prophets (with the exception of Muhammad). There is a huge divergence between Qur'anic and Biblical characters, doctrines, feasts, and events, a divergence that starts from the story of the Muslim Adam at the root of the tree, as we have observed. Thus supporting the conclusion that Allah and the LORD God are not the same.

Significance of the Islamization of Noah, Abraham, Moses and Jesus

Here we examine only the Anchor Prophets, but the same principle applies to all of them, i.e. their identities and messages have been incrementally but intentionally changed by omission, addition, denial, replacement, or by alteration and distortion.

In general, we will demonstrate that, in each case, the Qur'anic account provides some key "apparent similarities" with the Biblical account, thus providing the perception of continuity in line with the "sameness" claim.

These apparent similarities could be in the Islamized name, as well as in some key event or concept that seems to be the same.

Muslim Prophet Nooh (Noah)

The Differences Are Foundational

In the Islamic account[35] of the Islamized Noah, called Nooh[36], and compar-

---

35 The Qur'anic account of Nooh appears in bits and pieces in many places as in Surah's: 11:25-26, 29-32, 41, 43-46, 48; 17:3; 23:24, 27-29; 26:107, 116; 29:14; 69:12; 71:5-9, 23, 26-27.

36 In examining the name of Noah in Aramaic, it is also "Nooh." Hence there is some "sameness" in the name. But as will be demonstrated, the details are different.

ing it with the Biblical account[37], one discovers that although there are some apparent "similarities," in the flood story, there are however foundational differences and deviations which have major theological implications.

The Biblical account of the universal flood is rooted in the LORD God's process of fulfilling *His plan for salvation*. It consisted with the "painful" decision to eliminate all "wickedness" as this wickedness dominated the human race, but with the saving grace of preserving the "righteous blood line" through Noah, and then providing an unconditional "covenant" to Noah for all generations to come. The details of the Biblical account are very specific since they foreshadow Christ.

In contrast, the Qur'anic account creates a different narrative, a narrative based on eradicating the "unbelievers" in response to a request by Nooh. The rescue of Nooh, his family and some other believers is given as a process of preserving the Muslim "Ummah" and eradicating all kinds of apostasy.

Justification for the Flood

Let us compare the LORD God's justification for the flood with Allah's.

Looking at the Biblical account first, we learn that the LORD God was greatly "grieved" at the condition of mankind by the time Noah was born. Wickedness and sin became so prevalent that the LORD God decided to undo what he had started with the creation of Adam. But Noah found favor as he was not affected by this wickedness, and hence the LORD God provided an avenue to preserve human kind in order to fulfill the promise of bringing salvation through the Messiah. It was the LORD God's decision and plan of implementation. We see this expressed in:

> Genesis 6:5-8, "*5 The Lord saw how great the wickedness of the human race had become on the earth, and that every inclination of the thoughts of*

---

[37] The main Biblical account of the story of Noah is given in the Book of Genesis 5:28-10:32. It has the full detail of his genealogy, LORD God revelation and covenant with him and command to build the "Ark", the flood, and what happened after the flood, the Noahic Covenant, his descendants and their genealogies. In both the Old and New Testaments, the various characters and writers, like Moses, Jesus, Paul, Isaiah, 1 Peter 3:18 etc. would refer to the story of Noah and its relationship to the LORD God's promise of salvation.

the human heart was only evil all the time. 6 The Lord regretted that he had made human beings on the earth, and his heart was deeply troubled. 7 So the Lord said, 'I will wipe from the face of the earth the human race I have created—and with them the animals, the birds and the creatures that move along the ground—for I regret that I have made them.' **8 But Noah found favor in the eyes of the Lord.**"

The *Qur'anic account* is very different. Instead of focusing on the widespread wickedness within the human race prior to the time of Noah, the Qur'an states that all mankind up to the time of Nooh were Muslim, composed of one Muslim Ummah:

Surah 2:213, *"Mankind were one community (i.e. Ummah) and Allah sent prophets with good news and warnings …"*[38]

Of course Nooh himself was a Muslim prophet sent strictly to his people.

Surah 7:59, *"Indeed, we sent Nooh to his people and he said: 'O my people, worship Allah. You have no other god but him…'"*

According to Islamic sources, idol worship started at the time of Nooh, In fact the Qur'an provides the names of those idols in Surah 71 named "Surah of Nooh":

Surah 71:23, *"And they (idol worshippers of Nooh's day) said: 'You shall not desert your gods, nor shall you abandon Wadd, nor Suwaa', nor Yaghooth, nor Ya'ooq nor Nasr' (these are the names of their idols)."*

And hence Allah "sent him" to preach Islam.

Surah 10:71-72, *"**71.** And recite to them the news of Nooh. When he said to his people: 'O my people, if my stay, and my reminding of the signs of Allah is hard on you, then I put my trust in Allah. So devise your plot, you and your partners ….**72.** But if you turn away, then no reward have I asked*

---

38 According to [Ref. 24] the Hadith declares that mankind was Muslim up to the time of Nooh.

of you, my reward is only from Allah, and I have been commanded to be one of the Muslims.'"

As a result and after various attempts to "bring back" the people to Islam, Nooh gave up and asked Allah to destroy all the "Mushriks" (idol worshippers who associate other deities with Allah).

> Surah 71:26-27, "26 *And Nooh said: 'My Lord! Leave not one of the disbelievers on the earth!' 27 'If you leave them, they will mislead your slaves, and they will beget none but wicked disbelievers.'"*

There is no reference to Allah having been "grieved" by this idol worship, but rather that his decision to bring the flood was an immediate response to the request by his prophet Nooh.

The "Rescue" Process: Salvation?

In the Biblical account, the unilateral decision by the LORD God to execute a universal flood would lead to the commanding of Noah to build the "ark" with full details as to its dimensions, structure, materials to be used and method of construction (Genesis 6:15-21) and concluding in:

> Genesis 6:22 *"Noah did everything just as God commanded him,"*

with precise attention to detail:

> Genesis 7:1-5 *"1 The Lord then said to Noah, 'Go into the ark, you and your whole family, because I have found you righteous in this generation. 2 Take with you seven pairs of every kind of clean animal, a male and its mate, and one pair of every kind of unclean animal, a male and its mate, 3 and also seven pairs of every kind of bird, male and female, to keep their various kinds alive throughout the earth. 4 Seven days from now I will send rain on the earth for forty days and forty nights, and I will wipe from the face of the earth every living creature I have made." 5 **And Noah did all that the Lord commanded him.**'"*

The Bible continues with specific reference to times and dates as the flood began to recede:

Genesis 8:3-5, "**3** *The water receded steadily from the earth. At the end of the hundred and fifty days the water had gone down,* **4** *and on the seventeenth day of the seventh month the ark came to rest on the* **mountains of Ararat**[39]. **5** *The waters continued to recede until the tenth month, and on the first day of the tenth month the tops of the mountains became visible.*"

The details of disembarkation are also significant:

Genesis 8:6-12, "**6** *After forty days Noah opened a window he had made in the ark* **7** *and sent out a raven, and it kept flying back and forth until the water had dried up from the earth.* **8** *Then he sent out a dove to see if the water had receded from the surface of the ground.* **9** *But the dove could find nowhere to perch because there was water over all the surface of the earth; so it returned to Noah in the ark. He reached out his hand and took the dove and brought it back to himself in the ark.* **10** *He waited seven more days and again sent out the dove from the ark.* **11** *When the dove returned to him in the evening, there in its beak was a freshly plucked olive leaf! Then Noah knew that the water had receded from the earth.* **12** *He waited seven more days and sent the dove out again, but this time it did not return to him.*"

Upon disembarkation, Noah would build an altar to the Lord:

Genesis 8:13-20, "**13** *By the first day of the first month of Noah's six hundred and first year, the water had dried up from the earth. Noah then removed the covering from the ark and saw that the surface of the ground was dry.* **14** *By the twenty-seventh day of the second month the earth was completely dry.* **15** *Then* **God said to Noah,** **16** *'Come out of the ark, you and your wife and your sons and their wives.* **17** *Bring out every kind of living creature that is with you—the birds, the animals, and all the creatures that move along the ground—so they can multiply on the earth and be fruitful and increase in number on it.'* **18** *So Noah came out, together with his sons and his wife and his sons' wives.* **19** *All the animals and all the creatures that move along the ground and all the birds—everything that moves on land—came out of the ark, one kind after another.* **20** *Then Noah built an*

---

[39] According to scholars, Ararat means, "The curse has been reversed."

altar to the Lord and, taking some of all the clean animals and clean birds, **he sacrificed burnt offerings** *on it.'"*

Moving now to the Qur'anic account of Nooh story, it starts with back and forth interactions between Nooh and his people, in terms of ridiculing his building of a "ship", not an ark (Typologically Noah's Ark foreshadows Christ)[40]:

> Surah 11:38, *"And as he was constructing the ship, whenever the chiefs of his people passed by him, they made a mockery of him. He said: 'If you mock at us, so do we mock at you likewise for your mocking.'"*

The details of this "ship" are not mentioned. Instead we are told that as the flood started, Nooh and his family, plus possibly other "believers" boarded the ship and took with them (single) pairs of animals:

> Surah 11:40-41, *"**40.** (So it was) till then there came our command and the oven gushed forth (water like fountains from the earth). We said: 'Embark therein, of each kind two (male and female), and your family, except him against whom the word has already gone forth, and those who believe. And none believed with him, except a few.' **41.** And he [Nooh] said: 'Embark therein, in the name of Allah will be its moving course and its resting anchorage. ...'"*

The text above *"except him against whom the word has already gone forth"* refers to Qur'anic statements that one of Nooh's wives and one of his sons drowned as "Kafirs" (unbelieving apostates) along with the other unbelievers[41].

> Surah 11:42-43, *"**42.** So it (the ship) sailed with them amidst the waves like mountains, and Nooh called out to his son, who had separated himself (apart), 'O my son! Embark with us and be not with the disbelievers.' **43.** The son replied: 'I will betake myself to a mountain, it will protect me from the water.' Nooh said: 'This day there is no protector from the decree of Allah except him on whom he has mercy.' And a wave came in between them, so he (the son) was among the drowned."*

---

40 The Bible calls this vessel, the Ark. The Qur'an refers to it only as a "ship" ("Fulk" in Arabic). There is great significance to the concept of the Ark in the Bible, which is not there in the Qur'an.
41 The Qur'an does not give the name of his "son" who drowned. In the Sira there is speculation that his name was either Yad, or Kanaan.

Hence, even when Nooh would plead with Allah to rescue his son, Allah would refuse, declaring that a Kafir has nothing to do with Nooh's family[42]:

> Surah 11:45-46 "**45** *And Nooh called upon his Lord and said, 'O my Lord, my son is of my family! And certainly, your promise is true, and you are the most just of the judges.' 46He (Allah) said: 'O Nooh, surely, he is not of your family; his work is unrighteous, so ask not of me that of which you have no knowledge. I admonish you, lest you be one of the ignorant.'"*

The Qur'an gives an alternative and brief account of the disembarkation. After the flood and the recession of the waters, the ship would settle on "Mount Judi"[43]:

> Surah 11:44, "*And it was said: 'O earth. Swallow up your water, and O sky, stop the rain.' And the water was made to subside and the matter was accomplished, and the ship rested on Mount Judi[44], and it was said: 'Away with the unjust people (Kafirs, polytheists)'"*.

What Happened after the Rescue?

According to the Biblical account, after the rescue the LORD God would announce an unconditional "covenant" not to destroy all life again, despite the fact that man's sin nature was still there:

- Genesis 8:21, "*The Lord smelled the pleasing aroma (of the burnt offering given in [Gen. 8:20]) and said in his heart: 'Never again will I curse the ground because of humans, **even though every inclination of the human heart is evil from childhood**. And never again will I destroy all living creatures, as I have done.'"*

---

42 This is in anticipation of the doctrine of "Alwalaa' wal Baraa'" (Allegiance to Allah only and denouncing and renouncing "Kafirs", i.e. apostates)

43 According to Muslim official commentators, Mount Judi is in Mesopotamia near the city of Musol. See http://www.altafsir.com/Tafasir.asp?tMadhNo=0&tTafsirNo=74&tSoraNo=11&tAyahNo=44&tDisplay=yes&UserProfile=0&LanguageId=2

44 In the Bible the Ark would rest on the tallest mountain in the area, called Mount Ararat. Today, Mount Ararat is in eastern Turkey far away from where the Qur'anic Mount Judi is allegedly located near the city of Mosul in Iraq.

- Genesis 9:11-13, *"11 I establish my **covenant** with you: Never again will all life be destroyed by the waters of a flood; never again will there be a flood to destroy the earth. 12 And God said, 'This is the sign of the covenant I am making between me and you and every living creature with you, a covenant for all generations to come: 13 I have set my rainbow in the clouds, and it will be the sign of the covenant between me and the earth.'"*

But the BiblicalBiblical story does not end here. The entire account of Genesis 10 (the record of the descendants of Noah) and Genesis 11 (the tower of Babel) are not to be found in the Qur'an.

In contrast, the Qur'anic account ends with the rescue via the "ship" with no further continuity, other than that after Nooh, people started to deviate from Islam, thus necessitating further sending of messengers and prophets to call people back to "Islamic Monotheism."

Omissions, Replacements, Additions, Changes and Distortions

In comparing the Qur'anic vs. the Biblical accounts of the Noah/Nooh stories we summarize the issues as follows:

The original Biblical story of Noah demonstrates not only historical facts in precise detail, but provides some key markers and foreshadows for events to come, as expressed for example by Jesus Himself (Matt. 24:37-41), and in the Book of Hebrews (11:7). Some examples of these theologically significant foreshadowings are given herein, each of which is ultimately either countered or omitted in the Qur'anic version. However, our list is far from being exhaustive and does not provide a point-by-point comparison:

1. The LORD God Himself because of the worldwide spread of evil initiated the flood decision. He was deeply grieved about the state of man at that point, and found favor in one man, Noah, and his family to preserve the human race. This foreshadows the concept of "rebirth" which is foundational in Biblical Christianity.

2. The Bible provides very specific details about the Ark (not ship as in the Qur'an), its design, method of construction, even the materials used for the construction. The Ark is symbolic of Christ Himself as the source and means of our salvation.

3. The Bible also provides details about the flood itself, its duration, and eventually its end. These details are also critical in understanding typology and the foreshadowing of Christ (See Ref.'s 11, 17, 18 and 19):

   a. The number 40 is a repeated Biblical motif: The flood was complete in 40 days, after which Noah opened the window of the Ark. Note that Jesus fasted for 40 days. The Israelites spent 40 years in the desert, among many other examples.

   b. The number 7 is also symbolic: 7 pairs of each animal type, the Ark came to a place of rest on the 17th day of the 7th month. This is considered as a foreshadowing of the resurrection of Jesus, as the resurrection happened on that same day in the Jewish calendar.

   c. In the decision when to leave the Ark, Noah sends a raven and then a dove. These are foreshadowings of the doctrines of "law" (raven) and "grace" (dove).

4. Upon disembarking, Noah built an altar, and sacrificed animals in a burnt offering, thus affirming the blood sacrificial system, again another foreshadowing of the sacrifice on the cross.

5. The LORD God would make an unconditional covenant with Noah and his sons that He will never destroy the earth in another flood.

In sharp contrast, the Qur'anic story of the "Anchor Prophet" Nooh provides a different version of the "flood"—through deconstruction of the Biblical narrative, and its almost point-by-point replacement by the Islamic narrative—as derived from the Fitrah, the Tawheed and Muslimhood of all the prophets, to establish Muhammad's call for all mankind to return to the "original Islamic Monotheism". The following list provides examples of such Qur'anic countering of the Biblical narrative:

1. Until the time of Nooh all of humanity was "one Muslim Ummah" thus affirming the doctrine of the Fitrah and the Muslimhood of mankind.

2. Shirk (associating deities with Allah) started at the time of Nooh, thus causing Allah to send Nooh to bring the people back to Islam.

3. The call to destroy all of humanity was by a demand from Nooh to Allah to destroy all the idol worshipers, meaning "Mushriks" who associated other deities with Allah. [Ref.24]

4. The flood event established some important Islamic precedents to be further elaborated upon in various Islamic doctrines:

    a. Being a Muslim is not a matter of choice.

    • Surah 42:13, "*He (Allah) has ordained for you the same religion (Islam) which He ordained for Nooh, and that which we have inspired in you (O Muhammad), and that which we ordained for Ibrahim, Moosa, and Issa, saying you should establish religion, and make no divisions in it. Intolerable for those who associate partners with Allah, is that to which you (O Muhammad) call them. ...*"

    • Surah 3:83, "*Do they seek other than the religion of Allah, while to him submitted all creatures in the heavens and the earth, willingly or unwillingly...*"

    • Surah 3:85, "*And whoever desires a religion other than Islam - never will it be accepted from him, and in the hereafter, he will be among the losers.*"

    b. A Kafir (apostate) member of a family does not have any rights and is doomed to hell fire.

    c. Though being labeled an "Anchor Prophet" Nooh could not intercede for anyone, including his son.

    d. However, Allah would respond positively to Nooh when it came to the destruction of all opponents (The Kafirs)[45].

---

45 This tends to affirm what we will show in the next chapter about Allah's favors toward Muhammad.

e. After the flood the Muslim community (i.e. Ummah) was restored for a while, but the need for more prophets and messengers continued until the time of the "final messenger", Muhammad.

Muslim Prophet Ibrahim (Abraham)

The Myth of the "Three Abrahamic Religions"

In examining the Islamic account of the Islamized Abraham, renamed Ibrahim, and comparing it with the Biblical account of Abram and later Abraham, the main seeming resemblance between the two accounts is that of the concept of the "sacrifice of the son." Even then, the two "sacrifice" stories are vastly different in detail and, of course, in outcomes and concluding doctrines. All other aspects of the life stories of Abram/Abraham vs. Ibrahim, are strikingly different. Yet, it is the accepted norm for many Christian theologians and missiologists to refer to Judaism, Christianity, and Islam as the "three monotheistic Abrahamic religions," thus joining them together in one group that is distinct from other belief systems.

Strangely enough, the Qur'an unequivocally denounces any association of Ibrahim with Jews or Christians and their beliefs:

Surah 3:67, "*Ibrahim was neither a Jew nor a Christian, but he was a true Hanafi Muslim and he was not of those who associate partners with Allah.*"

Ibrahim and His Belief in Allah vs. the LORD God's Covenant with Abram/Abraham

The Ibrahim of Islam is depicted in the Qur'an in ways reminiscent of Muhammad's story. Having lived among idol worshiping pagans, Ibrahim would arrive at the belief in the one Allah through reason:

Surah 6:76-79, "*76 When the night covered him over, He saw a star: He said: 'This is my Lord.' But when it set, he said: 'I love not those that set.' 77 When he saw the moon rising in splendor, he said: 'This is my Lord.' But when the moon set, He said: 'unless my Lord guide me, I shall surely be among those who go astray.' 78 When he saw the sun rising in splendor, he said: 'This is my Lord;*

this is the greatest.' But when the sun set, he said: 'O my people! I am innocent of the charge of giving partners to Allah (i.e. Shirk). 79 'For me, I have set my face, firmly and truly, towards him who created the heavens and the earth, and never shall I give partners to Allah.'''

After "reasoning" that idols are to be rejected in preference to one Allah, Ibrahim has a number of confrontations with his unbelieving father[46], the pagan people of his time and his king[47]. And Allah would later miraculously save Ibrahim from being thrown into a fire because of his opposition to the idol worshippers of his time. (Surah 21:64-69)[48]

Consequently, Ibrahim would become a true example for Muslims:

> Surah 60:4, *"Indeed there has been an excellent example for you in Ibrahim (Abraham) and those with him, when they said to their people: 'We are free from you and whatever you worship besides Allah, we have rejected you, and there has started between us and you, hostility and hatred forever, until you believe in Allah only,' except the saying of Ibrahim (Abraham) to his father: 'I will ask for forgiveness (from Allah) for you, but I have no power to do anything for you before Allah Our Lord'..."*[49]

In fact, he is the only prophet who would share this honor with Muhammad of being a true example for mankind. Why is that? Islam tells us that Muhammad was the direct descendant of Ibrahim through his Muslim son Ismaeel (the Islamized name of Ishmael).

But there is more.

---

46 The Qur'an calls him "Azar" as compared with his Biblical name, "Terah".
47 Islamic traditions identify this king as "Namrud", the Islamic name of Nimrod.
48 Surah 21:66-69, *"Ibrahim said, 'Do you then worship, besides Allah, things that can neither be of any good to you nor do you harm?' 'Fie upon you, and upon the things that you worship besides Allah. Have you no sense?' They said, 'Burn him and protect your gods'. We said, 'O Fire, be cool, and safety for Ibrahim.'"*
49 This is reminiscent of the inability of Nooh to intercede for his son and another application that the "Kafirs" in one's Muslim family would go to hell. Note that in Islam, only Muhammad has the intercessory authority.

All of this is in opposition to the Biblical account whereby the LORD God revealed Himself directly the Abram first, and later to Abraham and made a covenant with him—a concept which is an anathema for Allah, as Allah only imposes covenants, and does not make covenants binding on himself. In Genesis 12:1-3 the Bible states:

> *"1 The Lord had said to Abram, 'Go from your country, your people and your father's household to the land I will show you. 2 "I will make you into a great nation, and I will bless you; I will make your name great, and you will be a blessing. 3 I will bless those who bless you, and whoever curses you I will curse; and all peoples on earth will be blessed through you.'"*

This initial covenant will be repeated and expanded when the LORD God changes his name from Abram (father of altitude) to Abraham (father of multitudes, many nations).

> Genesis 17:4-6, *"As for me, this is my covenant with you: You will be the father of a multitude of nations. No longer will your name be Abram. Instead, your name will be Abraham because I will make you the father of a multitude of nations. I will make you extremely fruitful. I will make nations of you, and kings will descend from you."*

Some of the key features of the "Abrahamic Covenant," are:

(a) It is an unconditional covenant.

(b) It involves the promise of the Savior, Christ Jesus, to be born from the "seed" of Abraham: Gal. 3:16, *"Now to Abraham and his Seed were the promises made. He does not say, 'And to seeds,' as of many, but as of one, 'And to your Seed,' who is Christ"*.

(c) It also involves the promise of the "land" to be given to his descendants through Isaac.

Furthermore, the foundation of the Christian doctrine of "Salvation by Grace", is related to Abraham. The Apostle Paul elaborates on this doctrine in Romans 4:3, *"What does Scripture say? 'Abraham believed God, and it was credited to him as righteousness'"*, thus echoing Genesis 15:6, *"Then he believed in the LORD; and He reckoned it to him as righteousness."*

This account focuses on the restoration of divine/human relationship by "electing" Abram/Abraham whereby through his "seed" Jesus Christ will be born of a virgin, with the full expression of the doctrine of salvation by grace emanating from Abraham's believing response to the LORD God's promise.

Divergence at the "Sacrifice" Episode

The Biblical story achieves one of its greatest pinnacles in the command by the LORD God to Abraham to sacrifice his son, Isaac. The foreshadows of the atonement through the blood sacrifice are familiar to the Christian reader. In Genesis 22:2 we read, "*Then God said, 'Take your son, your only son, whom you love—Isaac—and go to the region of Moriah. Sacrifice him there as a burnt offering on a mountain I will show you.*'" Note here that the intended "sacrifice" is for a "burnt offering", on Mount Moriah, of "***his only son.***" Of course the region of Moriah is where Jesus Christ would later on be crucified.

The alternative story of the "sacrifice" in the Qur'an achieves multiple Islamic purposes.

First, by requiring the sacrifice to be of Ismaeel rather than Is-haaq, Muhammad could then build the case for his "authority" by attaching himself to Ibrahim without being in the Hebrew line of prophets (Figure 2 of the Tree of the Prophets demonstrates that the branch from Ismaeel to Muhammad is distinct from the Hebrew branch that starts with Is-haaq).

Second, this attempted sacrifice would take place on an unnamed hill/mountain in "Mecca" rather than on Mt. Moriah (See Figure 3 showing the Islamic version of Ibrahim's travels).

Later when Ismaeel grew up, Ibrahim would join him again in Mecca to rebuild the Kaaba, the central shrine of Islam. This would then form the basis of the significant Islamic feast, the "Feast of the Sacrifice" (Eid Al-Adha) which in one fell swoop appropriates the Arab pagan tradition to Islam, links Muhammad to the Biblical traditions, and most importantly, provides the alternate theme and doctrine of denying the salvific sacrifice of Christ on the cross.

Later, Muhammad would declare the Kaaba in Mecca to be the most sacred shrine of Islam.

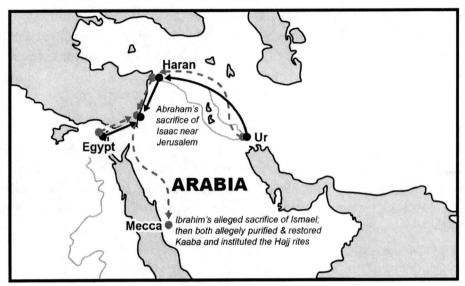

Figure 3: Abraham / Ibrahim, the fork in the road ... The re-routing of Biblical history. Journeys of Biblical Abraham (red) vs. journeys of Qur'anic Ibrahim (green).

Omissions, Replacements, Additions, Changes and Distortions

1. Added: Accepted imposed Fitrah covenant as given to Adam declaring all mankind born Muslim

2. Added: Accepted imposed Covenant of the Prophets declaring Muhammad to be the Seal of the Prophets

3. Omitted: Allah did not speak directly to Ibrahim

4. Omitted: Allah did not "call" Ibrahim

5. Changed: Was a Muslim prophet: "Ibrahim was neither a Jew nor a Christian, but a true Muslim..."(Surah: 3:67)

6. Changed: Sent to the idol worshippers of Ur, Haran, and Canaan

7. Added: Was a recipient of the "coming down" of 10 books from the Eternal Tablet of the Qur'an.

8. Omitted: Abrahamic covenants of blessings, seed, nations, and land.

9. Changed and replaced: Ibrahim's journey from Ur to Canaan and Egypt extended on to Mecca.

10. Changed and replaced: Abraham's sacrificial offering of Isaac on Mount Moriah, was replaced by Ibrahim's attempted sacrifice of Ismaeel in Mecca.

11. Changed and replaced: The Ismaeel "sacrifice" counters the atonement on the cross and replaces the meaning of "the Biblical sacrifice" with a symbolic Islamic test of obedience to Allah.

12. Added: Ibrahim and Ismaeel purified and restored/rebuilt the Kaaba in Mecca.

13. Added: Ibrahim instituted the Islamic Hajj rituals in Mecca, focusing on Ismaeel's sacrifice of obedience (countering the sacrifice of Isaac as a picture of substitutionary atonement and a foreshadow of the death and resurrection of Christ).

Muslim Prophet Moosa (Moses)

The Context of Moosa and the Jews

The Qur'an is replete throughout with verses and text with various episodes and commentaries on Moosa (Islamic name of Moses) and his constituency "the Jews (Al-Yahud in Arabic)" or "the Children of Israel, (Banu Isra'eel)". Moosa is mentioned by name 130 times, but the entire context of "the Jews" occupies almost 60% of the entire Qur'an[50]. Without much exaggeration, one would conclude that Muhammad and Allah, through the pages of the Qur'an and Hadith, are overwhelmingly preoccupied with the Jews and the underlying story of Moosa and his relationship with them. Therefore we should carefully examine the two narratives, the Biblical and Qur'anic, to establish the huge differences between the accounts, even though they are couched with apparent similarities.

The Biblical Account of Moses

The Biblical context of Moses is huge and foundational in understanding the full Biblical narrative of the LORD God's story of salvation and redemption. As quoted earlier, Jesus reminded his disciples of the scriptures, "*And beginning with Moses and all the Prophets, he explained to them what was said in all the Scriptures concerning himself.*" (Luke 24:27) He would continue, "*...Everything must be fulfilled that is written about me in the Law of Moses, the Prophets and the Psalms...*" (Luke 24:44)

---

[50] See the section entitled "Portrayal of the Jews in the Qur'an" (Page 34), of the book by Al-Maqdisi and Solomon, "Al-Yahud: Eternal Islamic Enmity and the Jews," ANM Publishers, 2010.

Moses, as the reported writer through the Holy Spirit of the first five books of the Bible, referred to either as the Pentateuch or the Torah, would explain his own story mainly in the Books of Exodus and Numbers, but "the Law" and the issues surrounding it are given in the remaining two books, Leviticus and Deuteronomy.

The main theme of the Moses story is within the context of the LORD God's fulfillment of His covenant with Abraham:

> Exodus 2:23-25, "**23** *During that long period, the king of Egypt died. The Israelites groaned in their slavery and cried out, and their cry for help because of their slavery went up to God.* **24** *God heard their groaning and he remembered his covenant with Abraham, with Isaac and with Jacob.* **25** *So God looked on the Israelites and was concerned about them.*"

An essential part of the "fulfillment" is not only the election of Moses, but of His people, the Jews and their return to the Promised Land. It is a story of the profound "revelation" of the LORD God both to Moses and His people. It is a story of salvation, grace, covenant—all within the context of the foreshadowings and typologies of Christ.

The Biblical Moses story consists of three segments: First 40 years in the palace of Pharaoh, the second 40 years in exile in Median, and the last 40 years leading his people through the struggle with Pharaoh, the Exodus from Egypt, and the preparation of God's people to enter the Promised Land. This story is a foreshadowing of the salvation available to each one of us through acceptance of Jesus Christ as Lord and Savior. And even after Christ came to us in the flesh and provided the final fulfillment of God's promise, and despite the rejection by the Jews of his time, the Bible declares through the Apostle Paul,

> Romans 11:1-2, "*I ask then: Did God reject his people? By no means! I am an Israelite myself, a descendant of Abraham, from the tribe of Benjamin.* **2** *God did not reject his people, whom he foreknew…*"

The Qur'anic/Islamic Narrative of Moosa and the Jews

Moosa, the Islamized Moses, has a historical narrative that seems similar to the Biblical one but with both stark and subtle differences that gradually chip away the trajectory of the Biblical narrative culminating in completely different conclusions.

The story line consists also of three segments with a notable difference: first 40 years in Pharaoh's palace, next 8 years (not 40 as in the Bible) in exile in Median, and the last 40 years in taking the Jews out of Egypt, preparing them to enter the Promised Land. By the end of the story and what would follow in terms of the opposition Moosa had faced from his followers, the Qur'an would at some point declare unequivocally the Jews as the permanent and eternal enemies of Allah[51] (In the particular Surah's below, "they" always refers to "the Jews"):

- Surah 2:61, " ... *They were covered with humiliation and misery; they drew on themselves the wrath of Allah. This is because they went on rejecting the signs of Allah and slaying his messengers without just cause. This is because they rebelled and went on transgressing...*"

- Surah 5:64, "...*We have put enmity and hatred amongst them till the day of resurrection. Every time they kindled the fire of war, Allah extinguished it; and they would strive to make mischief on earth. And Allah does not like the corruptors.*"

- Surah 62:6-7, "*6 Say (O Muhammad): "O you Jews! If you pretend that you are friends of Allah, to the exclusion of all other mankind, then long for death if you are truthful." 7 But they will never long for it (death), because of what (deeds) their hands have sent before them! And Allah knows well the unjust.*"

- Surah 5:82, "*You will truly find the most hostile of people to those who believe to be the Jews ...*"

Furthermore, although the Qur'an and Islam would portray Moosa as a Muslim "Anchor" prophet of great stature preaching the message of Islam, not only to his people but to Pharaoh and the people of Egypt, the Qur'an and Hadith would insert incidents in his story to lower his stature.

Portrayals of Moosa and his various encounters are scattered throughout the Qur'an making it difficult to piece together the entire narrative.

---

51 For much more details, see "Al-Yahud: Eternal Islamic Enmity and the Jews," by Al-Maqdisi and Solomon, ANM Publishers, 2010.

Differences between the Two Narratives

The differences between the Qur'anic/Islamic narrative of Moosa and that of the Biblical narrative of Moses, may be grouped into three categories: Omissions, additions and replacements/distortions. This would result in the implicit and explicit justification of Islamic "doctrines" all of which are in direct opposition to Christian doctrines and beliefs. We explore these in what follows:

1. **Omissions:** There is a host of omissions in the Qur'anic story of Moosa as compared with the Biblical one. We concentrate here on just a few of the notable ones:

   a. **The Passover**: The Biblical account of the Passover in Exodus 12, based on the decision by the LORD God to kill the first-born in all of Egypt, but to spare the children of Israel by painting their doorposts with the blood of the lamb they had killed in preparation for the Passover meal and the Exodus, is completely omitted from the Qur'anic text. There is a suggested good reason for that—the Passover is indeed a foreshadowing of death on the cross, an event that the Qur'an denies and opposes.

   b. **The Jewish Festivals**: The seven Jewish festivals are ignored. Christian theologians have established that four of these festivals (Passover, Unleavened Bread, First Fruits, and Pentecost), have already been fulfilled in Christ in the New Testament.[52] The final three festivals (Trumpets, the Day of Atonement, and Tabernacles) are yet to be fulfilled.

   c. **The Ten Commandments** (Exodus 20:1-17): They do not appear as such. Instead the Qur'an mentions the "tablets" Moosa received from Allah, but does not mention their contents. Surah 7:145, "*And we inscribed for him in the tablets about all things, as an admonition and a detailing of all things...*'"

   d. **The Five Offerings prescribed by Leviticus**: 1-7: All these five offerings are fulfilled in the Sacrifice of Christ. [Ref. 15]

---

52 See :http://www.gotquestions.org/Jewish-feasts.html#ixzz3F80HmNgM

1. Burnt Offering,

2. Meal Offering,

3. Peace Offering,

4. Sin Offering, and

5. Trespass Offering.

e. **The Tabernacle**: this foundational foreshadowing of Christ is fully omitted from the Qur'anic text. In comparison the Book of Exodus devotes Chapters 25 through 28 to provide the precise design of the Tabernacle. [See Ref. 's 13 and 14 for the significance of the design of the Tabernacle]

f. **The Mosaic Covenant**: This "conditional" covenant is essential to understanding the LORD God's purposes and eventual fulfillment of the "Law" through Jesus Christ. (Matt. 5:17-20)

g. **The Priesthood**: The Bible through Moses defines the priests to be Levites consisting of Aaron, his sons and their descendants. It also defines their roles, dress, and duties. Christ would then replace the Aaronic priesthood as our only "Priest."

h. **Presence of God with His people**: The physical presence of God in the form of "pillar of fire and a cloud" are not represented as such in the Qur'an. Although the shading of his people by cloud is mentioned, but it is only an element of nature, not the presence of God.

2. **Qur'anic "additions" and "changes":**

a. Moosa accepted imposed Fitrah covenant as given to Adam declaring all mankind born Muslim

b. Moosa gave testimony of himself as being a Muslim, "*And Moses said, 'O my people, if you have believed in Allah, then rely upon him, if you should be Muslims.'*"(Surah 10:84)

c. Moosa accepted the imposed "Covenant of the Prophets" imposed by Allah to accept Muhammad as the "Seal of the Prophets" (Surah 3:81)

d. Moosa preached Islam to Pharaoh, "*And Moosa said, 'O Pharaoh, I am a messenger from the Lord of the worlds.'*" (Surah 7:104)

e. The magicians/sorcerers converted to Islam and were crucified by Pharaoh, according to (Surah 26:45-51)

f. Pharaoh would finally believe in Allah only as he was drowning, according to Surah 10:90"*And We took the Children of Israel across the sea, and Pharaoh and his soldiers pursued them in tyranny and enmity until, when drowning overtook him, he said, 'I believe that there is no deity except that in whom the Children of Israel believe, and I am of the Muslims.'*"

g. The Qur'anic episode of Moosa and Al-Khidr: This is reported in Surah 18:66-78 and is elaborated upon in the Hadith and the Sirah. This rather convoluted episode attempts to lower the status of Moosa by putting him to the test by an unknown prophet called Al-Khidr to counter Moosa's claim that he was the most knowledgeable of the prophets.

h. All of Moosa's followers are declared Muslims: "*And Moosa said: 'O my people! If you have believed in Allah, then put your trust in Him if you are Muslims'*" (Surah 10:84)

3. **Replacements/Distortions:**

a. Departing of the children of Israel from Egypt in secret (Surah 26:52-57). In contrast with the Bible whereby Pharaoh had initially given his "permission" for the children of Israel to "go." (Ex. 12:31)

b. Moosa, instead of writing the Tawrat, it "came down" to him from the Eternal Tablet.

Muslim Prophet Issa (Jesus)

The Context of Issa in Islam

The Qur'anic/Islamic narrative regarding the Muslim Prophet Issa, son of Maryam, is the crux of the answer to our question, "Is the Allah of Islam One and the same as the LORD God of the Bible?" For if the answer were to be "Yes" then Islam would be in agreement with the Biblical Triune God: Father, Son and Holy Spirit. But this is not the case.

In the Qur'an Issa is mentioned by name 25 times, and there are over 90 Ayah's/verses associated with him directly. Also, the indirect references to Issa and Christians (termed Nasara), are far more numerous than that. Furthermore, there are hundreds, if not thousands, of episodes and stories associated with Issa given in the Hadith, the Sirah and other Islamic traditions. [Ref. 27]

The Muslim Issa was Born of a Virgin

The Islamic narrative about Issa emphasizes that he was a "Muslim Anchor Prophet" who was born of a virgin (Maryam), but was a created being[53], not the Son of God. He was given the role of a prophet from birth, but his mission would start when he became an adult as a prophet and messenger to the Jewish people, with no mention of his age at that point in time. The Qur'anic story of the virgin birth contains some apparent similarities to the account given in the Gospel of Luke, Chapters 1 and 2, but there are major differences in detail and in the Qur'anic interpretation of events associated with these details.

The main "virgin birth" narrative is given in Surah's 19 and 3. Here are some excerpts:

1. Maryam's Encounter with Jibril:

   - Surah 19:16-21, "*16. And mention in the book (the Qur'an), the story of Maryam, when she withdrew in seclusion from her family to a place facing east. 17. She placed a screen (to screen herself) from them; then we sent to her our spirit (Jibril), and he appeared before her in the form of a man in all respects. 18. She said: 'I seek refuge with the most beneficent from you, if you do fear Allah.' 19. He said: 'I am only a messenger from your Lord, to announce to you the gift of a righteous son.' 20. She said: 'How can I have a son, when no man has touched me, nor am I unchaste?' 21. He said: 'Your Lord said: 'That is easy for me, and to appoint him as a sign to mankind and a mercy from us, and it is a matter decreed.'*"

---

[53] See Surah 3:59, "*The likeness of Issa in Allah's sight, is that of Adam. He created him of dust, and to him, 'be', and he would be.*"

- Surah 3:45 *"When the angels said: 'O Maryam, Allah gives you the glad tidings of a word from him, his name will be the Messiah Issa, the son of Maryam, held in honor in this world and in the hereafter, and will be one of those who are near to Allah.'"*

2. Issa Born under a Palm Tree

Surah 19:22-23, "**22.** *So she conceived him, and she withdrew with him to a far place.* **23.** *And the pains of childbirth drove her to the trunk of a date palm. She said: 'Would that I had died before this, and had been forgotten and out of sight!'"*

3. Issa, the Baby in the Cradle Defends Himself and His Mother

Surah 19:24-31, "*24. Then a voice cried unto her from below, saying: 'Grieve not, your Lord has provided a water stream under you; 25. 'And shake the trunk of date palm towards you, it will let fall fresh ripe-dates upon you.' … 27. Then she brought him (the baby) to her people, carrying him. They said: 'O Mary! Indeed you have brought an amazing thing. … 29. Then she pointed to him. They said: 'How can we talk to one who is a child in the cradle?' 30. 'He (Issa) said: I am a slave of Allah, he has given me the scripture and made me a prophet; 31. And he has made me blessed wherever I be, and has enjoined on me Salat (prayer), and Zakat, as long as I live. 32. And dutiful to my mother, and made me not arrogant. 33. And peace be upon me the day I was born, and the day I die, and the day I shall be raised alive'"*

The "Word", the "Spirit" and the Explicit Rejection of the Trinity

Despite the use of the expression that Issa was a "Word" from Allah with a "Spirit" from Allah bestowed unto him, the Qur'an denies any form of divine nature associated with Issa and attacks a version of the "trinity" as a form of polytheism and "Shirk" (associating partners with Allah), which is the ultimate blasphemy in Islam. The Islamic version of the "trinity" is in the form of an accusation that Christians believe in three gods: Allah, Issa, and Maryam.

Surah 4:171, "*O people of the Scripture (Jews and Christians)! Do not exceed the limits in your religion, nor say of Allah aught but the truth. The Messiah Issa, son of Maryam, was (no more than) a messenger of Allah and his word, which he bestowed on Maryam and a spirit (Ruh)created by him; so believe in Allah and his messengers. Say not: 'Three' Cease! It is better for you…"*

Surah 3:59 explains the term " a word" as referred to above in Surah 4:171, as not being "the Word" as referred to in the Gospel of John, but instead is the direct command, **"be"** by Allah to *create* Issa, "*The likeness of Issa before Allah is the likeness of Adam. He created him from dust, then said to him: 'Be!' - and he would be."* [54]

In the same vein, the use of the term "spirit" is not in reference to the "Holy Spirit", the third person of the holy trinity, but is rather "a spirit."

Miracles, Shariah and Mission of Issa

Though said to be only a man, Issa is elevated to the status of a major Muslim prophet who carried out many miracles, and made changes to the Jewish dietary laws. As such, some of his reported miracles are exaggerated and unfounded with no evident purpose.

Issa would put life into a bird from clay, as follows:

> Surah 3:49-50, "**49***And I will make him (Issa) a messenger to the children of Israel (saying): 'I have come to you with a sign from your Lord, that I design for you out of clay, as it were, the figure of a bird, and breathe into it, and it becomes a bird **by Allah's leave**; and I heal him who was born blind, and the leper, and I bring the dead to life **by Allah's leave**. And I inform you of what you eat, and what you store in your houses. Surely, therein is a sign for you, if you believe.' **50** And I have come confirming that which was before me of the Tawrat (Torah), and to make lawful to you part of what was forbidden to you, and I have come to you with a proof from your Lord. So fear Allah and obey me."*

The important qualifier, "by Allah's leave" (note in bold above) is used consistently by Muslims to assert that all the miracles of Issa were from Allah, and not from him, as he was just a prophet with no power of his own. Surah 13:38 amplifies this even further:

---

54 Muslim translators/commentators would translate this expression as "… he created him from dust and *then said to him: 'Be!' - and he **was***" instead of what the actual Arabic states, "*Be and it would be.*"

Surah 13:38 states, "*And indeed we sent messengers before you (O Muhammad), and made for them wives and offspring. And it was not for a messenger to **bring a sign except by Allah's leave**...*"

Note that this rather bizarre and ostentatious "miracle" by Issa is not a reflection of the character of the Jesus of the Bible but is used in the Qur'an to make the case that this and the other miracles all came by permission from Allah. Some Christian missionaries; however, take this example to try to establish that the Qur'an recognizes the divinity of Issa.

The elevation of Issa would culminate in his central "mission" which was to declare the coming of "Ahmad" (one of Muhammad's names),

Surah 61:6, "*And when Issa, son of Maryam (Mary), said: 'O Children of Israel! I am the messenger of Allah unto you confirming the Tawrat which came before me, and giving **glad tidings of a messenger to come after me,** whose name shall be Ahmed'...*'"

Consequently, Issa and his disciples would preach Islam:

Surah 3:52, "*Then when Issa came to know of their disbelief (i.e. the Jews), he said: 'Who will be my helpers in Allah's cause?' The disciples said: 'We are the helpers of Allah; we believe in Allah, and bear witness that we are Muslims.'*'"

The above Qur'anic quotations establish the identity of the Issa of the Qur'an—defining who he was and what he did. The sections below will clarify the Islamic position of who he was and was not. This is achieved by categorically denying foundational aspects of the identity of the Jesus of the Bible.

Issa Was not Crucified

According to the Qur'anic account the confrontation between Issa and the Jewish establishment, the Jews would plot to kill him with no specific reason being given other than their evil nature. Yet Allah, in his "mercy and protection" of his prophet, would intervene directly. Rather than allowing Issa to be crucified, he would allow a person who resembled Issa to be crucified in his stead and would lift Issa up to himself, with the expectation being given that later on he (Issa) would return to earth to complete his "mission" of refuting Christianity and establishing Islam.

The Qur'an asserts that the "plot" by the Jews to kill Issa was outmaneuvered by Allah, who is the "best of the plotters":

> Surah 3:54, "*And they (the Jews) plotted (to kill Issa), and Allah plotted too (to rescue him). And Allah is the best of the plotters.*"

So Allah prevented the crucifixion by placing Issa's likeness on another man:

> Surah 4:157, "*And because of their saying, 'We killed Messiah Issa, son of Maryam, the Messenger of Allah,' - but they killed him not, nor crucified him, but the resemblance of Issa was put over another man, and those who differ therein are full of doubts. They have no knowledge, they follow nothing but conjecture. For surely; they killed him not.*"

Instead, Allah raised Issa to himself:

> Surah 4:158, "*But Allah raised him (Issa) up unto himself...*"

The Qur'an goes on to assert that once "raised up unto himself", Allah would cleanse Issa of error and prepare him for the message he would bring in his so-called, "second coming."

> Surah 3:55, "*Allah said, 'O Issa, I will take you and raise you to myself and purify you from those who disbelieve and make those who follow you (i.e. the Muslims) superior to those who disbelieve until the day of resurrection. Then to me is your return, and I will judge between you concerning that in which you used to differ.'*"

Second Coming of Issa

Issa's mission during his second coming would be to bring all the Christians who had "gone astray" by believing in his deity, back to the true doctrine of the "Original Islamic Monotheism"(Tawheed). He would manifest this by breaking the cross (the most hated symbol of Islam), and by killing the pig (the most rejected food in the Islamic dietary laws). As a human, he would then get married, have children, die, and be buried next to Muhammad in Medina.

What Will Happen on Judgment Day?

The Qur'an also reports, that on the Last Day, Allah would rebuke Issa by interrogating him regarding the issue as to whether he, Issa, had commanded his followers to worship him and his mother alongside himself. As a humiliated human being, Issa would then declare his limited understanding and lack of perception beyond what Allah had revealed to him, renouncing any responsibility for "Christians" having elevated him to the level of a partner, hence divine, and further confessing his lack of any authority to intercede for his followers, thus petitioning Allah to deal with them as he, Allah, would see fit:

> Surah 5:116-118, "*116Andwhen Allah will say: 'O Issa, son of Maryam, **did you say to men: Worship me and my mother as two gods besides Allah?'** Issa will reply: 'Glory be to you. It was not for me to say what I had no right (to say). Had I said such a thing, you would surely have known it. You know what is in my inner self though I do not know what is in yours, truly, only you, are the all-knower of all that is hidden and unseen. 117 Never did I say to them except what you (Allah) did command me to say: 'Worship Allah, my Lord and your Lord.'* And I was a witness over them while I dwelt amongst them, but when you took me up, you were the watcher over them, and you are a witness to all things.'"118 If you punish them, they are your servants: If you forgive them, you are the exalted in power, the wise."*

Comparison of the Qur'anic Account of Issa with the Biblical Narrative of Jesus

1. Changed: Issa was a "created being", like Adam by a command of Allah through miraculous virgin birth (not incarnated)—Surah 3:59, Surah 19:16-33.

2. Denied: Was neither the Son of God, nor was He God.

3. Changed: Only a prophet, and sent to the Jews only.

4. Added: Accepted imposed Fitrah covenant as given to Adam declaring all mankind born Muslim.

5. Added: Accepted imposed covenant to declare Muhammad as the Seal of the Prophets.

6. Added: Recipient of the "coming down" of a book, called "The Injeel" (Gospel) from the Eternal Tablet of the Qur'an.

7. Added: Given a "Shariah" (which was incomplete).

8. Added: He made changes to dietary laws, i.e. made some forbidden foods permitted (Halal).

9. Denied: Was not crucified, but was "lifted" to heaven.

10. Added: Main mission: Messenger to the children of Israel (only),to prophecy the coming of Muhammad (Surah 61:6).

11. Added: On the Last Day Allah will humiliate "prophet Issa" by interrogating him as to whether he made himself and his mother out to be gods. In response, Issa will deny it and will relinquish any responsibility for his followers giving him divine status.

12. Added: Issa will say to Allah, "If you choose to punish them, do so." By this he declares that he has no intercessory authority.

Chapter 5
So, Who Is Allah?

The Dilemma within Islam

Having answered the question from the perspective of whether or not Allah is one and the same, or even tangentially similar to the LORD God of the Bible with a resounding "no", the question remains—then who is he?

In this chapter we explore the central dilemma that has faced Muslim scholars throughout Islamic history—the dilemma of defining the *nature of Allah* or more precisely in developing the so-called, *Doctrine of Allah*, while proclaiming that he *never* reveals his nature, so his nature cannot be known and that any attempt to do so is considered the highest level of Shirk (i.e. association of any deity or person with Allah).

They would develop the terms, (a) "Tawheed", meaning absolute oneness or unity to describe Allah[55] and (b) "Tanzeeh", meaning that Allah is free of all anthropomorphisms and absolutely incomparable to anything or anyone, in other words being pure and distinct from all associations (see Figure 4). They would then state that Tawheed is the "true monotheism" from the foundation of the universe.

They would use Qur'anic verses and Hadith quotations to denounce the triune God of the Bible as violating both the Tawheed and the Tanzeeh, and would produce as evidence a distorted definition of the "Trinity" calling it "Shirk". Islam teaches that the "Trinity" is composed of three gods. There is a school of thought that posits that this trinity is composed of Allah, Maryam and Issa, inferring a physical union between Allah and Maryam. Even when explained that this is not the case, but that the Biblical doctrine of the trinity is rather Father, Son, and Holy Spirit; the Muslim scholars would still regard it as polytheism and associating partners with Allah (Shirk). Despite being unable to tell us anything of substance about Allah, they still object and continue to vehemently refute the Biblical doctrine of the self-revealing Triune God.

---

55 See Appendix A on the "Coinage of the Tawheed Term."

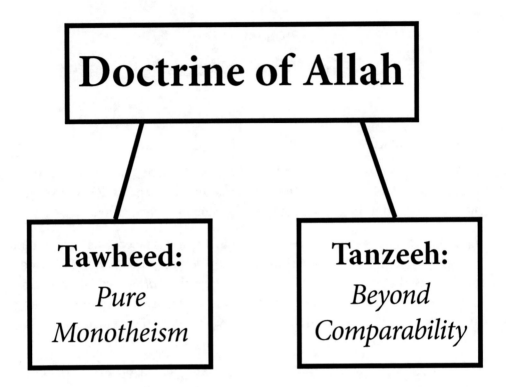

Figure 4: Islamic Doctrine of Allah with its two major components, Tawheed and Tanzeeh.

The history of the development of the doctrine of Allah in Islam contains a wide range of irreconcilable concepts. Scholars such as the Sufi (mystical) Ibn Arabi, had come to the conclusion, based on his deduction from the primary sources that *"Allah is all and all is Allah."* He laid down this voluminous landmark teaching in his treatise entitled "Al Futuhat al Makkiya," among other works. Ibn Arabi's works and especially "Al-Futuhat" remain until today in great demand and in circulation all over the Islamic world and are studied by Muslim scholars. However, in reality one must face the conclusion that Ibn Arabi actually preached and taught a pantheistic notion of Allah.[56]

Other prominent Muslim scholars took different directions. For example Wasil Ibn Atta[57] taught that although Allah was indeed everywhere and in everything, neither Allah was all, nor all was Allah. Wasil ibn Atta belonged

---

56 In Al-Ftuhat Al-Makkiah Ibn Arabi states, "… in the last analysis, Allah Himself is the spirit of the cosmos, while the cosmos is His body."
57 See for example http://www.muslimphilosophy.com/hmp/13.htm

to an 8th century (AD) rationalistic school of Islamic thought known as the Mu'tazilites. It was the Mu'tazilites who were instrumental in developing various key Islamic disciplines and systems, many of which continue to influence Islam today. Yet another eminent scholar like Ibn Taymiyyah declared both of the above two scholars as "Kaffirs" or "apostates".

Although Ibn Taymiyyah and many other leading scholars provided alternative derivations of the nature and meaning of Tawheed, all of them without exception used this same non-Qur'anic term, "Tawheed".[58] This term is not found anywhere in the Qur'an, though it is reported to have been coined and used by Muhammad himself.[See Appendix A for a discussion on the coinage of the Tawheed term].

In an interesting comparison between various Islamic schools, we make reference to an important opinion by Shaykh Muhammad Saalih al-Munajjid[59]. Without getting into the complex Islamic terminologies in that opinion, he makes reference to the works of important Muslim scholars and their schools of thought—all of whom attempted to deal with the Tawheed and its various aspects. These are referenced in the following footnotes: [60],[61],[62],[63].

Eventually the consensus of Muslim scholars would converge on three categories of the "Tawheed"[64][65]: (1) Lordship Tawheed, (2) Worship Tawheed and (3) Names/Attributes Tawheed. These three categories or classifications are and have been accepted to be foundational, interlinked, interdependent and inseparable. Anyone who does not hold to these classifications is termed as "Kaffir", an unbeliever /or a form of apostate.

---

58 See http://islamqa.info/en/10262

59 http://islamqa.info/en/205836

60 https://en.wikipedia.org/wiki/Abu_Mansur_al-Maturidi#cite_note-9

61 https://en.wikipedia.org/wiki/Abu_Mansur_al-Maturidi#cite_note-10

62 https://en.wikipedia.org/wiki/Abu_Mansur_al-Maturidi#cite_note-11

63 https://en.wikipedia.org/wiki/Abu_Mansur_al-Maturidi#cite_note-12

64 See, Muhammad Bin Abdel-Wahhab, *Collected Works—Volume 1: Tawheed Book*, ISBN 10 Ddgit: 0-9825133-7-2 (2010, in Arabic)

65 See also, Abu-Ameenah Bilal Philips, *The Fundamentals of Tawheed (Islamic Monotheism)*, International Islamic Publishing House, (ISBN 9960-850-99-4)

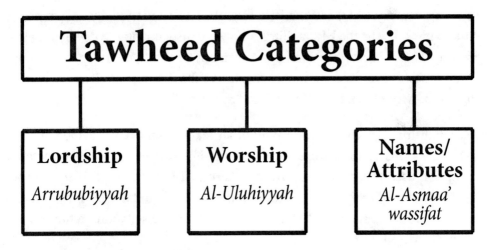

Figure 5: The three-pronged approach to defining Tawheed

But before explaining these three categories, it is important to note that Muslim scholars have also emphasized the need to establish a framework of limitations which provide necessary boundary conditions on the three categories, i.e. all of the three categories of Tawheed have to be consistent with and governed by these limitations.

Framework of the Doctrine of Allah Establishes His "Limitations"

Based on the Tanzeeh doctrine (i.e. Allah is beyond comparability in all manners), but also on other ancillary but connected arguments, Muslim scholars have managed to establish a framework to define the doctrine of Allah. In Figure 6, the boundary limitations to follow are illustrated in a manner of "framing" the three categories of Tawheed mentioned above to be detailed later in this chapter.

Thus although Allah is said to be all-powerful, all-present, and all-knowing, there are "primary boundaries," consisting of four major aspects that must be avoided in describing him[66]. These boundaries evolved over several centuries of deliberations and debates, but eventually became the driver of any further discussions on the subject. These four boundaries of avoidance are termed:

---

66 The information given regarding these four items id based in part on the well-accepted Fatwa and opinion source: http://islamqa.info/en/34630

1. Tahreef (No Distortion): Total prohibition on changing, or even questioning the "meaning", of any Qur'anic text that refers toAllah's attributes.

2. Ta'teel (No Omission of Allah's Names): Denial that any of Allah's attributes can be set aside.

3. Tamtheel/Tashbeeh (Negation of Anthropomorphism): Denial that Allah can be likened or compared to anything.

4. Takyeef (Negation of "How"): Denying of man's ability to describe "how" Allah achieves his purposes.

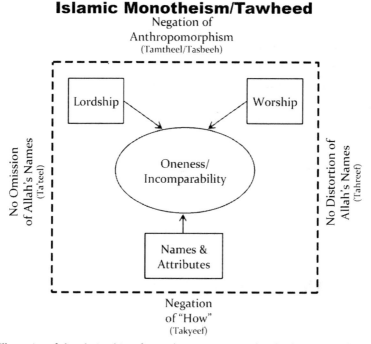

Figure 6: Illustration of the relationships of terms/concepts associated with Islamic Monotheism (Tawheed)

Let's explain in some detail each one of these terms:

1. The *Tahreef* (No Distortion) aspect implies that the "meaning" of any Qur'anic text cannot be changed or distorted. An example of this distortion is that some scholars would "distort the meaning of the hand of Allah which is mentioned in many (Qur'anic) texts and say that it

refers to his blessing or power."[67] As we shall see later, humans are not in a position to provide meaning to the "Hand of Allah", as Allah is beyond any likeness to any human form. Even the attempt to describe or characterize his "hand" as conveying a blessing or as exhibiting power is suspect, and is considered to be a form of Tahreef, a distortion which is unacceptable.

2. The *Ta'teel* (No Omission of Allah's Names) aspect refers to "denying the beautiful names and sublime attributes and saying that Allah does not possess them or some of them." Thus although a *human* meaning cannot be given to Allah's "names and attributes" (according to the above Tahreef prohibition) any denial of their existence is prohibited, since Allah himself allegedly revealed them in the Qur'an.

3. The *Tamtheel/Tashbeeh* (Negation of Anthropomorphism) means that likening the attributes of Allah to the attributes of a human being is prohibited, such as saying that Allah mounted the throne as per Surah 13:2, "*Allah it is who raised up the heavens without visible supports, then mounted the throne ...*". Muslim scholars, and in particular the Mu'tazilites asked:

    a. "How" did he mount the throne?

    b. Did he mount the throne as a man would mount?

    c. Does this mean that positionally, the "timeless" Allah entered the time zone?

    d. If Allah mounted the throne, where was he before mounting the throne?

    e. Was Allah standing, and if he was standing, did he stand like a man?

    f. If Allah sits or mounts the throne, is the throne greater?

    g. Who is greater, the throne or Allah?

    h. Does this mean that Allah has a body of some form? Etc.

---

[67] Such as Surah 3:73, "*...Say: 'All bounties are in the **hand** of Allah...*'", Surah 48:10, "*...The **hand** of God is above their hands...*", or Surah 36:83, "*So glory be to him (Allah) in whose **hand** is the dominion of all things and to whom you will be returned*".

These deliberations led to various schisms which were finally settled by Al-Ghazali in his famous poem on the issue whereby he wrote, "Bila Kaif wala tashbeeh" (Without "how?" and without "likeness"). Al-Ghazali argued his position quoting many Qur'anic passages, with particular emphasis on Surah 42:11, *"There is nothing like Him..."*

Ibn Arabi commenting on Surah 55:27, *"But will abide (for ever) the face of thy Lord ..."* or 2:115, *"...there is the face of Allah..."* expounded on the anthropomorphism concept and posited that the "face of Allah" is literal. For that opinion he was severely criticized by other Muslim scholars.

This would extend to any form of likeness (called *Tashbeeh*), such as creating man in Allah's image, walking with Adam in the Garden, or most especially the Incarnation and Indwelling of the Holy Spirit according to the Bible. Hence the overall and all-encompassing aspect of the doctrine of Allah called *Tanzeeh*, as described above.

4. Finally, the *Takyeef* (Negation of "How") means discussing, questioning or speculating as to what the attributes of Allah are and how they are attained, whereby a person tries to give them verbal or pictorial image or description. This course of inquiry is strictly forbidden, as such understanding is said to be well beyond the capacity of human beings, according to Surah 20:110, *"but they will never encompass **anything** of his knowledge"*.

These aspects of the doctrine of Allah have come to be the standard measure by which the authoritative community of scholars have put an end to any attempt to give any meaning to the nature of Allah, as they consider doing that to be apostasy—although expressed outwardly in seemingly positive terms. These doctrines emanate from the principle of "who Allah is not"[68] rather than "who he is", as he/Allah is ultra-transcendent, relationless and utterly unknowable. In essence, they would establish Allah's limitations as will be discussed below.

In short, the four boundaries of Tahreef (no distorting), Ta'teel (no omission of Allah's names), Tamtheel/Tashbeeh (negation of anthropomorphism), and Takyeef (negation of "how") work together to prohibit any discussion of self-revelation or the knowability of Allah.

---

68 This is consistent with the philosophical concept of "via negative" discussed earlier.

As a result and after centuries of deliberation, Muslim scholars would converge on the "three categories of Tawheed" whereby they would employ these negative avoidance boundaries while providing an apparent positive description of the Tawheed. So what are the categories of Tawheed?

The Three Categories of Tawheed

We now consider the three categories of Tawheed, i.e. the oneness and unity of Allah (See Figure 5). These are:

1. Tawheed Arrububiyya (Lordship Tawheed): meaning maintaining the oneness of Allah.

2. Tawheed al Uluhiyya, better known as Tawheed Al-Ibada (Worship Tawheed): meaning, maintaining unity of worship.

3. Tawheed al Asmaa' wa-Assifaat (Names/Attributes Tawheed): meaning maintaining the unity of Allah's names and attributes

Before delving into the details of these categories, it is important to note that the above-mentioned classifications of Tawheed are accepted and upheld by all Sunni schools within the house of Islam.

However, the inseparability of Muhammad and Allah, and the indispensability of Muhammad's role, are crucial factors in understanding and upholding these three categories. In reality, no Islamic doctrine or concept can be understood without Muhammad's central role in the Tawheed doctrine. This emerges only when the details of each category are explained.

In what follows, we provide explanations of these three categories based on what the Muslim scholars have established.

Tawheed Arrububiyya (Lordship Tawheed)

Tawheed Arrububiyya (Lordship Tawheed) means upholding or maintaining the unity of Allah as master or sovereign, i.e. Lord (Rab, in Arabic). He is solely the one and only and has no partners. This means that Allah is the sole creator of everything, master of the universe and all that inhabits it. He is the sustainer of all, imparting death and life (Surah 67:2, "*He who created death and life* ..."), disposer of affairs of mankind, judge, rewarder and punisher of them at the judgment day. The following are some Qur'anic references in this regard:

- Surah 39:62, "*Allah is the creator of all things, and he is the guardian and disposer of all affairs.*"

- Surah 37:96, "*But Allah has created you and your handwork*"

Many believe that Muhammad's contemporary pagan Arabs did not know that the supreme being had created all the universe and that he is the sustainer of life, and that Muhammad was the first to preach this oneness of Allah as the god of Islam. In truth that was not the case at all. The Qur'an states that the pagan Arabs knew and believed in a supreme being called "Allah":

- Surah 43:87, "*If you ask them (pagan Arabs), who created them, they will certainly say, Allah: How then are they deluded?*"

- Surah 29:63, "*And if indeed you ask them who is it that sends down rain from the sky, and gives life therewith to the earth after its death, they will certainly reply, 'Allah'...*"

So the pagan Arabs of Muhammad's time knew about Allah as the lord and the master creator of the universe, the sustainer of life and giver of all good things:

Surah 10:31, "*Say: 'Who is it that sustains you (in life) from the sky and from the earth? Or who is it that has power over hearing and sight? And who is it that brings out the living from the dead and the dead from the living? And who is it that rules and regulates all affairs?' They (pagan Arabs) will soon say, 'Allah. Say, 'Will you not then show piety?'*"

And in times of trouble they cried out to Allah:

Surah 31:31-32, "*Don't you see that the ships sail through the ocean by the grace of Allah? That he may show you of his signs? In this are signs for all who constantly persevere and give thanks. When a wave covers them like the canopy, they (pagan Arabs) call to Allah, offering him sincere devotion. But when he has delivered them safely to land, there are among them those that would waiver. But none reject our signs except only one who is treacherous and ungrateful*".

According to the foregoing Qur'anic references, it has been clearly demonstrated that many of the pagan Arabs knew and believed in the supreme creator Allah, that he is the sustainer and the disposer of their affairs. He is the one who sends them rain, and he controls the seasons, and when in trouble they will call upon him to be delivered. And when asked, "Who created you?" they would say, "Allah". But despite that, Allah of the Qur'an declares them to be unbelievers as they rejected Muhammad and his claims.

Muslim scholars presentations and explanations of the **Lordship Tawheed** (Rububiyyah) are shrouded to present the uniqueness of Allah, acknowledging yet minimizing the intrinsic role of Muhammad. However many of them have openly expounded this with its corollary concepts imbedded in the doctrines of Al-Walaa' wal-Baraa' [Ref. 4][69] and the doctrines associated with the rights of Muhammad. [Ref. 20]

In reality **Lordship Tawheed** (Rububiyyah) demands that people believe in the finality of Muhammad alongside the utter unity of Allah, and whosoever of the pagans did not pronounce allegiance audibly by confessing the Shahadah (which links Allah and Muhammad), was put to death. Muhammad said:

> *"I have been sent with a sword and no man will escape my sword until he recites the Shahadah."*[70]

In other words, despite the pagans' beliefs in Allah as the creator and sustainer of the universe, and their calling upon him at times of trouble—yet without confessing the Shahadah, Allah would regard them as Kaffirs, for they would not have believed and publicly acknowledged Muhammad as the final messenger.

Tawheed Al-Ibada (Worship Tawheed)

According to the Qur'an, the sole purpose of Allah in the creation of Jinn and mankind is for them to serve and worship Allah as per Surah 51:56, "*I (Allah) have only created Jinns*[71] *and men, that they may worship (serve) me ...*" This Ayah establishes the basis for *Tawheed Al-Ibada (Worship Tawheed)*. Not only is Allah "Lord" according to "Lordship Tawheed", but he is to be worshiped, or more accurately, to be served.

---

69 This doctrine as explained in [Ref. 4] requires the Muslims to show allegiance to Islam and demonstrate rejection and outward enmity to non-Muslims.
70 This is a slight variation of Hadith 1:33, Sahih Muslim
71 See the section below that describes the Jinn.

Now this worship, service or "Ibada" (in Arabic) cannot be performed in anyway one chooses. It has to be practiced exactly as laid down by Muhammad, individually or corporately, be it in Salat (the ritual prayers), in Sawm (Ramadan fasting), in Zakat (religious tax for Muslims), in the Hajj (pilgrimage to Mecca), in Jihad, in Nikah (contracted marriage partnership), as well as in the upholding of all the "Halal" (whatever is allowed) and the "Haram" (whatever is prohibited).

According to Islamic understanding, no amount of serving and worshipping of Allah alone would be acceptable, for a person must believe in Allah and Muhammad equally according to Surah's 24:62 and 49:15:

- 24:62, "*The true believers are only those who sincerely believe in **Allah and in his messenger**...*"

- 49:15, "*Only those are believers **who have believed in Allah and his messenger**, and have never since doubted, but have striven with their belongings and their persons in the cause of Allah: Such are the sincere ones.*"

- 48:13, "*And whosoever **does not believe in Allah and his messenger**, then we have prepared for the disbelievers a blazing fire.*"

So to recite or believe only the first part of the Shahadah, "*No deity but Allah ...*", is insufficient, and neither makes a person a Muslim, nor makes him acceptable to Allah and he/she remains in the fold of Kufr (i.e. unbelief or apostasy).

Instead, a person must believe and uphold the second part of the Shahadah, "*... and Muhammad is the messenger of Allah*", thus establishing that Muhammad is the final messenger of Allah and is superior over all other messengers. Only then one is regarded as upholding Tawheed.

However, if one were to regard the two parts of the creed as separate categories one would be declared as a Mushrik (an unbeliever/apostate).

Only when one upholds and believes that the entire Shahadah (composed of two statements merged as one), then and only then, one is regarded as having upheld the Tawheed.

Further, not only has Allah commanded belief in both himself and in Muhammad, but obedience to Muhammad *is* obedience to Allah, according to:

Surah 4:80, *"He who obeys the messenger has already obeyed Allah ..."*

Figures 7 and 8 demonstrate that, because of the Shahadah, one cannot become a Muslim without believing in both Allah and Muhammad. They are inseparable. The figure also demonstrates that denial of Allah (or associating partners with him) is "Kufr," and is the unforgivable sin. Denial of Muhammad is also "Kufr" (blasphemy).

To conclude, Worship Tawheed (upholding or maintaining the unity of worship) is unachievable without Muhammad, the messenger of Allah. This extends to every aspect of a Muslim's life individually, corporately and as part of the Islamic community. For the pinnacle of Worship Tawheed is only achieved by obeying both Allah and Muhammad.

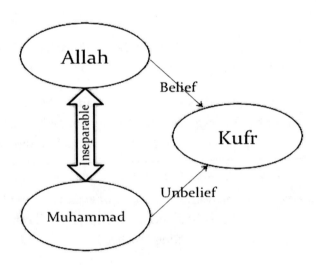

Figure 7: Believing in Allah while denying Muhammad is Kufr

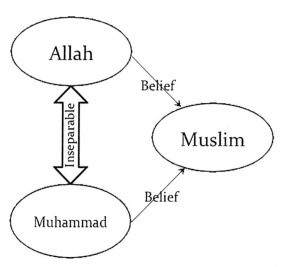

Figure 8: Only when one believes in both Allah and Muhammad jointly that he/she becomes a Muslim

Tawheed Al-Asmaa' Wa al-Sifat (Names/Attributes Tawheed)

Muslims worldwide take great pride in the so-called 99 names of Allah. They are usually framed and displayed prominently in their homes and businesses.

First, let's look at some Qur'anic references about the 99 names:

- Surah 17:110-111, "**110.** *Say (O Muhammad): 'Invoke Allah the most beneficent, by whatever name you invoke him, it is the same, for to him belong the best names. ...'***111.** *And say: 'All the praises and thanks be to Allah, who has not begotten a son, and who has no partner in his dominion, nor would he need anyone to protect him from humiliation, and **magnify him with all the magnificence**.'"*

- Surah 59:22-24, "**22.** *He is Allah, none has the right to be worshipped but he, the all-knower of the unseen and the seen. He is the most beneficent, the most merciful.* **23.** *He is the king, the holy, the one free from all defects, the giver of security, the watcher over his creatures, the all-mighty, the compeller, the supreme. Glory be to Allah above all that they associate as partners with him.* **24.** *He is Allah, the creator, the inventor of all things, the bestower of forms. To him belong the best Names. All that is in the heavens and the earth glorify him. And he is the all-mighty, the all-wise."*

- Surah 20:8, "*Allah. No god but he. To him belongs the most beautiful name*"

Table 1 gives the Arabic transliteration of these names together with their translation into English.[72] These names/attributes have been compiled from various Qur'anic verses. Among Muslim scholars there were some differences of opinion about this issue. However, in the final analysis, the scholars have agreed upon the list shown below.

Table 1: List of the 99 names/attributes of Allah

Allah	Allah	AR-RAHMÂN	The Compassionate	AR-RAHÎM	The Merciful
AL-MALIK	The King	AL-QUDDÛS	The Most Holy	AS-SALÂM	The All-Peaceful,
AL-MU'MIN	The believer	AL-MUHAYMIN	The Protector	AL-'AZÎZ	The Mighty
AL-JABBÂR	The Compeller	AL-MUTAKABBIR	the proud one/the prideful	AL-KHÂLIQ	The Creator
AL-BÂRI'	The Maker	AL-MUSAWWIR	The Bestower of form, Shaper	AL-GAFFÂR	The Forgiver
AL-QAHHÂR	The Subduer	AL-WAHHÂB	The Bestower	AR-RAZZÂQ	The Provider
AL-FATTÂH	The Opener, The Judge	AL-'ALÎM	The All-Knowing	AL-QÂBID	The Withholder
AL-BÂSIT	The Expander	AL-KHÂFID	The Abaser	AR-RÂFI'	The Exalter
AL-MU'IZZ	The Bestower of honour	AL-MUDHILL	The Humiliator/the one who misleads	AS-SAMÎ'	The All-Hearing
AL-BASÎR	The All-Seeing	AL-HAKAM	The Judge	AL-'ADL	The Just, The Equitable
AL-LATÎF	The Gentle, The Knower of subtleties	AL-KHABÎR	The All-Aware	AL-HALÎM	The Forbearing
AL-'AZÎM	The Incomparably Great	AL-GAFÛR	The Forgiving	ASH-SHAKÛR	The Appreciative/the thankful one
AL-'ALIYY	The Most High	AL-KABÎR	The Most Great	AL-HAFÎZ	The Preserver
AL-MUGHÎTH	The Sustainer	AL-HASÎB	The Reckoner	AL-JALÎL	The Majestic, The Revered, The Sublime

---

72 Source with our corrections: http://www.islamicity.com/Mosque/99names.htm

AL-KARÎM	The Generous	AR-RAQÎB	The Watchful	AL-MUJÎB	The Responsive
AL-WÂSI'	The All-Encompassing, The All-Embracing	AL-HAKÎM	The Wise	AL-WADÛD	The Kind One
AL-MAJÎD	The Most Glorious	AL-BÂ'ITH	The Resurrector	ASH-SHAHÎD	The Witness
AL-HAQQ	The Truth	AL-WAKÎL	The Ultimate Trustee, The Disposer of Affairs	AL-QAWIYY	The Most Strong
AL-MATÎN	The Firm One, The Authoritative	AL-WALIYY	The Protector	AL-HAMÎD	The All-Praised, The Praiseworthy
AL-MUHSÎ	The Reckoner	AL-MUBDI'	The Originator	AL-MU'ÎD	The Restorer to life
AL-MUHYÎ	The Giver of life	AL-MUMÎT	The Causer of death	AL-HAYY	The Ever-Living
AL-QAYYÛM	The Self-Existing by Whom all subsist	AL-WÂJID	The Self-Sufficient, The All-Perceiving	AL-MÂJID	The Glorified
AL-WÂHID	The One	AS-SAMAD	The Eternally Besought	AL-QÂDIR	The Omnipotent, The Able
AL-MUQTADIR	The Powerful	AL-MUQADDIM	The Expediter	AL-MU'AKHKHIR	The Delayer
AL-AWWAL	The First	AL-ÂKHIR	The Last	AZ-ZÂHIR	The Manifest
AL-BÂTIN	The Hidden	AL-WÂLÎ	The Governor, The Protector	AL-MUTA'ÂLÎ	The Most Exalted
AL-BARR	The righteous	AT-TAWWÂB	The Granter and Accepter of repentence	AL-MUNTAQIM	The Lord of Retribution, The Avenger
AL-'AFUWW	The Pardoner	AR-RA'ÛF	The Most Kind, The Clement	MÂLIK-UL-MULK	Owner of the Kingdom
DHUL JALÂL WAL IKRÂM	Possessor of Majesty and Honour	AL-MUQSIT	The Just, The Equitable	AL-JÂME'	The Gatherer
AL-GHANIYY	The All-Sufficient	AL-MUGHNÎ	The Enricher	AL-MÂNI'	The Preventer of harm
AD-DÂRR	The Afflicter	AN-NÂFI'	The Benefiter	AN-NÛR	The Light

AL-HÂDÎ	The Guide	AL-BADÎ'	The Originator	AL-BÂQÎ	The Everlasting
AL-WÂRITH	The Ultimate Inheritor	AR-RASHÎD	The Guide	AS-SABÛR	The Patient One

The main issue that faced Muslim scholars was to establish meanings or under-standings of these names. What does it mean that Allah is called "Al-Rahim" (The Merciful), or "Al-Wahhab" (The Bestower)? What does it mean that he is "Al-Lateef" (The Gentle One), "Al-Jabbar" (The Compeller), or even "Al-'Aleem" (The All Knowing)?

After centuries of debates, and in order to avoid the various blind alleys of Qur'anic logic, Muslim scholars arrived at the four prohibition boundaries as explained earlier.

For example, prohibition boundary (1) is called: Tahreef (no distortion of Allah's names), that is, total prohibition on changing the "meaning" of any Qur'anic text. Hence, any human cannot come up with any meaningful defi-nition of these names/attributes. Yet, according to boundary (2): Ta'teel (no omission of Allah's names), no one is allowed to deny the existence of these. Even more limiting is boundary (3): (Tamtheel/Tashbeeh (negation of anthro-pomorphism) whereby although these names/attributes are human-like, the Qur'an asserts in Surah 42:11, *"There is nothing like Him .."* And to make it impenetrable, boundary (4): Takyeef (negation of "how") i.e. discussing how the attributes are attained, or even speculating about them, is considered to be far beyond human understanding according to Surah 20:110, *"but they will never encompass **anything** of his knowledge"*.

These four boundaries have been accepted and imposed by notable Islamic institutions. Thus, Muslim scholars have generally accepted:

1. That all negations of Allah must be seen as emphasizing his unique-ness rather than implying non-existence, according to Surah 42:11, *"... there is **nothing whatever like unto him**..."*

2. Although many of the names and attributes may be obviously human or anthropomorphic, Allah's character and being must not be human-ized, as required by the four boundaries.

3. Conversely, when similar attributes are given to men they cannot be "divinized".

Based on this, one has to accept Allah's names/attributes at face value without the ability to understand or even come close to comprehending their meaning, especially as one considers the "four boundaries" and the Doctrine of Tanzeeh.

But Islam has a clean way out of this impasse. If one cannot comprehend Allah's names and attributes, one can easily understand Muhammad's. Although Allah officially has 99 names/attributes, Muhammad has a lot more, ranging from 99 even up to 1000 names.[73]

Generations of Muslims have compiled lists of names of Muhammad. In the table to follow we provide a sampling of such names.

Upon taking a thorough look at these names and their variations from diverse Islamic sources, there is one glaring result. Many of those names are indistinguishable from Allah's names. But here is the reality of the matter: Since Allah is limited within his boundaries and one cannot understand or question the meaning of his names/attributes, Muhammad is just a "man" and one can fully understand the meaning of his names.

The following corresponds to one of the compilations of Muhammad's names.

Table 2: Names/Attributes of Muhammad [74]

1	Muhammad: Praised One.	2	Ahmad: Most Deserving of Praise.
3	al-Ahsan: The Most Beautiful. The Best.	4	Udhun khayr: Friendly Ear.
5	al-A`la: The Highest (in all creation).	6	al-Imam: The Leader.
7	al-Amin: The Dependable.	8	al-Nabi: The Prophet.

---

[73] See for example, https://en.wikipedia.org/wiki/Names_and_titles_of_Muhammad, among many other references on the subject.

[74] Source: http://www.alahazrat.net/islam/416-exalted-names-of-the-prophet-salalahualaihiwasalam.php#

9	al-Ummi: Literate without being taught by a Teacher -or- Base / Foundation of the Universe -or- the First & the Foremost..	10	Anfas al-'arab: The Most Precious of the Arabs.
11	Ayatullah: The Sign of Allah.	12	Alif lam mim ra: A-L-M-R.
13	Alif lam mim sad: A-L-M-S	14	al-Burhan: The Proof.
15	al-Bashir: The Bringer of Good Tidings.	16	al-Baligh: The Very Eloquent One.
17	al-Bayyina: The Exposition.	18	Thani ithnayn: The Second of Two.
19	al-Harîs: The Insistent One.	20	al-Haqq: The Truth Itself.
21	Ha Mim: H-M.	22	Ha Mim 'Ayn Sîn Qaf: H-M-'-S-Q.
23	al-Hanif: The One of Primordial Religion.	24	Khatim al-nabiyyin: The Seal of Prophets.
25	al-Khabir: The Knowledgeable One.	26	al-Da'i: The Summoner.
27	Dhu al-quwwa: The Strong One.	28	Rahmatun li al-'alamin: A Mercy for the Worlds.
29	al-Ra'uf: The Gentle One.	30	al-Rahim: The Compassionate One.
31	al-Rasul: The Messenger.	32	Sabil Allah: The Path to Allah.
33	al-Siraj al-munir: The Light-Giving Lamp.	34	al-Shâhid: The Eyewitness.
35	al-Shahîd: The Giver of Testimony.	36	al-Sâhib: The Companion.
37	al-Sidq: Truthfulness Itself.	38	al-Sirat al-mustaqim: The Straight Way.
39	Tah Sîn: T-S.	40	Tah Sîn Mim: T-S-M.
41	Tah Ha: T-H.	42	al-'Amil: The Worker.
43	al-'Abd: The Slave.	44	'Abd Allah: Allah's Slave.
45	al-'Urwat al-wuthqa: The Sure Rope.	46	al-'Aziz: The Mighty One. The Dearest One.

47	al-Fajr: The Dawn.	48	Fadl Allah: Allah's Grace.
49	Qadamu Sidq: Truthful Ground.	50	al-Karim: The Generous One.
51	Kaf Ha' Ya' 'Ayn Sad: K-H-Y-'-S	52	al-Lisan: Language Itself.
53	al-Mubashshir: The Harbinger of Goodness.	54	al-Mubîn: The Manifest.
55	al-Muddaththir: The Cloaked One.	56	al-Muzzammil: The Enshrouded One.
57	al-Mudhakkir: The Reminder.	58	al-Mursal: The Envoy.
59	al-Muslim: The One Who Submits.	60	al-Mashhud: The One Witnessed To.
61	al-Musaddiq: The Confirmer.	62	al-Muta`: The One Who Is Obeyed.
63	al-Makîn: The Staunch One.	64	al-Munadi: The Crier.
65	al-Mundhir: The Admonisher.	66	al-Mizan: The Balance.
67	al-Nas: Humanity.	68	al-Najm: The Star.
69	al-Thaqib: The Sharp-Witted One.	70	al-Nadhîr: The Warner.
71	Ni`mat Allah: Allah's Great Favor.	72	al-Nur: The Light.
73	Nun: N.	74	al-Hadi: Guidance Itself.
75	al-Wali: The Ally.	76	al-Yatim: The Orphan. The Unique One.
77	Ya Sîn: I-S.	78	âkhidh al-sadaqat: The Collector of Alms.
79	al-âmir: The Commander.	80	al-Nâhi: The Forbidder.
81	al-Tâli: The Successor.	82	al-Hâkim: The Arbitrator.
83	al-Dhakir: The Rememberer.	84	al-Râdi: The Acquiescent.
85	al-Râghib: The Keen.	86	al-Wâdi`: The Deposer.
87	Rafî` al-dhikr: The One of Exalted Fame.	88	Rafî` al-darajât: The One of The Exalted Ranks.

89	al-Sâjid: The Prostrate.	90	al-Sâbir: The Long-Suffering.
91	al-Sâdi`: The Conqueror of Obstacles.	92	al-Safuh: The Oft-Forgiving.
93	al-`âbid: The Worshipful.	94	al-`âlim: The Knower.
95	al-`Alîm: The Deeply Aware.	96	al-`Afuw: The Grantor of Pardon.
97	al-Ghâlib: The Victor.	98	al-Ghani: The Free From Want.
99	al-Muballigh: The Bearer of News.	100	al-Muttaba`: He Who Is Followed.
101	al-Mutabattil: The Utter Devotee.	102	al-Mutarabbis: The Expectant One.
103	al-Muhallil: The Dispenser of Permissions.	104	al-Muharrim: The Mandator of Prohibitions.
105	al-Murattil: The Articulate.	106	al-Muzakki: The Sanctifier.
107	al-Musabbih: The Lauder.	108	al-Musta`îdh: The Seeker of Refuge.
109	al-Mustaghfir: The Seeker of Forgiveness.	110	al-Mu'min: The Believer. The Grantor of Safety.
111	al-Mushâwir: The Consultant.	112	al-Musalli: The Prayerful.
113	al-Mu`azzaz: The Strengthened One.	114	al-Muwaqqar: Held in Awe.
115	al-Ma`sum: Immune.	116	al-Mansur: The One With Divine Help.
117	al-Mawla: The Master of Favors and Help.	118	al-Mu'ayyad: The Recipient of Support.
119	al-Nâsib: The One Who Makes Great Effort.	120	al-Hâdi: The Guide.
121	al-Wâ`izh: The Exhorter.	122	Ajîr: The Saved One.
123	Uhyad: The Dissuader.	124	Ahhad: The Peerless One.
125	Akhumakh: Of Sound Submission.	126	al-Atqa: The Most Godwary.
127	al-Abarr: The Most Righteous One. The Most Pious One.	128	al-Abyad: The Fairest One.

129	al-Agharr: The Most Radiant One.	130	al-Anfar: The One With the Largest Assembly.
131	al-Asdaq: The Most Truthful.	132	al-Ajwad: The Most Bounteous.
133	Ashja' al-Nas: The Most Courageous of Humanity.	134	al-âkhidh bi al-hujuzât: The Grasper of Waist-Knots.
135	Arjah al-nas 'aqlan: The Foremost in Humankind in Intellect.	136	al-A'lamu billah: The Foremost in Knowledge of Allah.
137	al-Akhsha lillah: The Foremost in Fear of Allah.	138	Afsah al-'arab: The Most Articulate of the Arabs.
139	Aktharu al-anbiya'i tabi'an: The Prophet With The Largest Following.	140	al-Akram: The One Held in Highest Honor.
141	al-Iklil: The Diadem.	142	Imam al-nabiyyin: The Leader of Prophets.
143	Imam al-muttaqin: The Leader of the God wary.	144	Imam al-nas: The Leader of Humankind.
145	Imam al-khayr: The Good Leader.	146	al-Amân: The Safeguard.
147	Amanatu as-habih: (The Keeper of) His Companions's Trust.	148	al-Awwal: The First.
149	al-âkhir: The Last.	150	Ukhrâya: The Last (of the Prophets). His name in the Torah.
151	al-Awwâh: The One Who Cries Ah.	152	al-Abtahi: The One from Bitah between Mecca and Mina.
153	al-Bâriqlît, al-Barqalîtos: The Paraclete. The Spirit of Holiness. The Innocent One.	154	al-Bâtin: The Hidden One (in his station).
155	Bim'udhma'udh: One of his names in the Torah.	156	al-Bayan: The Exposition.
157	al-Taqi: The One Who Guards Himself.	158	al-Tihami: The One from Tihama (the lowland of the Hijaz).
159	al-Thimal: The Protector.	160	al-Jabbar: The Fierce One.
161	al-Khatim: The Sealer.	162	al-Hâshir: The Gatherer.
163	Hât Hât: His name in the Psalms.	164	al-Hâfizh: The Preserver.
165	Hâmid: Praiseful.	166	Hâmil liwa' al-hamd: Bearer of the Flag of Praise.

167	Habib Allah: Allah's Beloved.	168	Habib al-Rahman: The Beloved of the Merciful.
169	Habîtan: His name in the Injil.	170	al-Hujja: The Proof.
171	Hirzan li al-'ayn: A Barrier Against The Evil Eye.	172	al-Hasîb: The Sufficient One. The Highborn One.
173	al-Hafîzh: The Keeper and Guardian.	174	al-Hakîm: The Wise One.
175	al-Halîm: The Meek One.	176	Hammitâya: Guardian of Sanctity.
177	al-Humayd: The Praised One.	178	al-Hamîd: The Praised One.
179	al-Hayy: The Living One.	180	Khâzin mal Allah: Allah's Treasurer.
181	al-Khâshi`: The Fearful One.	182	al-Khâdi`: The Submissive One.
183	Khatîb al-nabiyyin: The Orator Among the Prophets.	184	Khalil Allah: Allah's Close Friend.
185	Khalifat Allah: Allah's Deputy.	186	Khayr al-'alamin: The Greatest Goodness in the Worlds.
187	Khayru khalq Allah: The Greatest Good in Allah's Creation.	188	Khayru hadhihi al-umma: The Best of This Community.
189	Dar al-hikma: The House of Wisdom.	190	al-Dâmigh: The Refuter (of Falsehoods).
191	al-Dhikr: The Remembrance.	192	al-Dhakkar: The One Who Remembers Much.
193	al-Râfi`: The Exalter.	194	Râkib al-buraq: The Rider of the Buraq.
195	Râkib al-jamal: The Rider of the Camel.	196	Rahmatun muhdat: Mercy Bestowed.
197	Rasul al-rahma: The Emissary of Mercy.	198	Rasul al-raha: The Emissary of Relief.
199	Rasul / Nabi al-malahim: The Emissary / Prophet of Battles.	200	Rukn al-mutawadi`in: The Pillar of the Humble Ones.
201	al-Rahhab: The Most Fearful.	202	Ruh al-haqq: The Spirit of Truth.
203	Ruh al-qudus: The Spirit of Holiness.	204	al-Zahid: The One Who Does-Without.
205	al-Zaki: The Pure One.	206	al-Zamzami: The Heir of Zamzam.

207	Zaynu man wâfa al-qiyama: The Ornament of All Present on the Day of Judgment.	208	Sabiq: Foremost.
209	Sarkhatilos: Paraclete (in Syriac).	210	Sa'id: Felicitous.
211	al-Salam: Peace.	212	Sayyid al-nas: The Master of Humanity.
213	Sayyid walad Adam: The Master of the Children of Adam.	214	Sayf Allah: Allah's Sword.
215	al-Shâri': The Law-Giver.	216	al-Shâfî': The Intercessor.
217	al-Shafî': The Constant Intercessor.	218	al-Mushaffa': The One Granted Intercession.
219	al-Shâkir: The Thankful One.	220	al-Shakkâr: The One Who Thanks Much.
221	al-Shakur: The Ever-Thankful.	222	Sâhib al-taj: The Wearer of the Crown.
223	Sâhib al-hujja: The Bringer of The Proof.	224	Sâhib al-hawd: The Owner of the Pond.
225	Sâhib al-kawthar: The Owner of the River of Kawthar.	226	Sâhib al-hatîm: The Lord of the Court Before the Ka'ba.
227	Sâhib al-khâtim: The Owner of the Seal.	228	Sâhibu Zamzam: The Owner of Zamzam.
229	Sâhib al-sultan: The Possessor of Authority.	230	Sâhib al-sayf: The Bearer of the Sword.
231	Sâhib al-shafa'at al-kubra: The Great Intercessor.	232	Sâhib al-qadib: The Bearer of the Rod.
233	Sâhib al-liwa': The Carrier of the Flag.	234	Sâhib al-mahshar: The Lord of the Gathering.
235	Sâhib al-mudarra'a: The Wearer of Armor.	236	Sâhib al-mash'ar: The Owner of the Landmark.
237	Sâhib al-mi'raj: The One Who Ascended.	238	Sâhib al-maqam al-mahmud: The One of Glorified Station.
239	Sâhib al-minbar: The Owner of the Pulpit.	240	Sâhib al-na'layn: The Wearer of Sandals.
241	Sâhib al-hirâwa: The Bearer of the Cane.	242	Sâhib al-wasila: The Possessor of the Means.
243	Sâhib la ilaha illallah: The Teacher of "There is no god but Allah."	244	al-Sadiq: The Truthful.
245	al-Masduq: The Confirmed.	246	al-Sâlih: The righteous one.

247	al-Dâbit: The One Given Mastery.	248	al-Dahuk: The Cheerful One.
249	al-Tahir: The (Ritually) Pure One.	250	Tâb Tâb: Of Blessed Memory. His Name in the Torah.
251	al-Tayyib: The Salutary One. The Fragrant One.	252	al-Zhahir: The Prevailer.
253	al-`âqib: The Last in Succession.	254	al-`Adl: The Just.
255	al-`Arabi: The Arabian. The Speaker of Arabic.	256	`Ismatullah: Allah's Protection.
257	al-`Azhim: The Tremendous One.	258	al-`Afif: The Chaste One.
259	al-`Ali: The High One.	260	al-Ghafur: The Frequent and Abundant Forgiver.
261	al-Ghayth: Rain. Help (esp. in the elements).	262	al-Fâtih: The Conqueror.
263	al-Fâriq: The Separator Between Good and Bad.	264	Fârqilîta: The Paraclete.
265	Fartt: The Scout.	266	al-Fasîh: The Highly Articulate One.
267	Falâh: Felicity.	268	Fi'at al-muslimin: The Main Body of the Muslims.
269	al-Qa'im: The One Who Stands and Warns. The Establisher.	270	Qâsim: The Distributer.
271	Qa'id al-khayr: The Leader Who Guides to Goodness.	272	Qa'id al-ghurr al-muhajjalîn: Leader of the Bright-Limbed Ones.
273	al-Qattal: The Dauntless Fighter.	274	Qutham: Of Perfect Character. Gifted With Every Merit.
275	Qudmâya: The First (of the Prophets). His name in the Torah.	276	al-Qurashi: The One From Quraysh.
277	al-Qarîb: The Near One.	278	al-Qayyim: The Righteous Straightener (of the Community).
279	al-Kâff: The One Who Puts a Stop (to Disobedience).	280	al-Mâjid: The Glorifier.
281	al-Mâhi: The Eraser (of Disbelief).	282	al-Ma'mun: The One Devoid of Harm.
283	al-Mubarak: The Blessed One.	284	al-Muttaqi: The Godwary One.

285	al-Mutamakkin: Made Firm and Established.	286	al-Mutawakkil: Completely Dependent Upon Allah.
287	al-Mujtaba: The Elect One.	288	al-Mukhbit: The Humble Before Allah.
289	al-Mukhbir: The Bringer of News.	290	al-Mukhtar: The Chosen One.
291	al-Mukhlis: The Perfectly Sincere One.	292	al-Murtaja: The Much Anticipated One.
293	al-Murshid: The Guide.	294	Marhama: General Amnesty.
295	Malhama: Great Battle.	296	Marghama: Greater Force.
297	al-Musaddad: Made Righteous.	298	al-Mas`ud: The Fortunate.
299	al-Masîh: The Anointed.	300	al-Mashfu`: Granted Intercession.
301	Mushaqqah / Mushaffah: Praised One.	302	al-Mustafa: The One Chosen and Purified.
303	al-Muslih: The Reformer.	304	al-Mutahhir / al-Mutahhar: The Purifier / The Purified One.
305	al-Muti`: The Obedient One.	306	al-Mu`ti: The Giver.
307	al-Mu`aqqib: The One Who Comes Last in Succession.	308	al-Mu`allim: The Teacher.
309	al-Mifdal: The Most Generous.	310	al-Mufaddal: Favored Above All Others.
311	al-Muqaddas: The One Held Sacred.	312	Muqim al-Sunna: The Founder of The Way.
313	al-Mukrim: The One Who Honored Others.	314	al-Makki: The Meccan One.
315	al-Madani: The Madinan One.	316	al-Muntakhab: The Chosen One.
317	al-Munhaminna: The Praised One (in Syriac).	318	al-Munsif: The Equitable One.
319	al-Munib: The Oft-Repentant One.	320	al-Muhajir: The Emigrant.
321	al-Mahdi: The Well-Guided One.	322	al-Muhaymin: The Watcher.
323	al-Mu'tamin: The One Given the Trust.	324	Mûsal: Mercied. (In the Torah.)

325	Mâdh Mâdh / Mûdh Mûdh / Mîdh Mîdh: Of Blessed Memory.	326	al-Nâsikh: The Abrogator.
327	al-Nâshir: The Proclaimer.	328	al-Nâsih: The Most Sincere Adviser.
329	al-Nâsir: The Helper.	330	Nabi al-marhama: The Prophet of General Amnesty.
331	al-Nasîb: The One of High Lineage.	332	al-Naqiy: The Limpid One.
333	al-Naqîb: Trustee. Guarantor.	334	al-Hâshimi: The One of Hâshim's Line.
335	al-Wâsit: Central in Relation To All The Noble Families.	336	al-Wâ`id: The Harbinger of Terrible News.
337	al-Wasîla: The Means.	338	al-Wafi: Holder of His Promise.
339	Abu al-Qasim: Father of Qasim.	340	Abu Ibrahim: Father of Ibrahim.
341	Abu al-Mu'minin: Father of the Believers.	342	Abu al-Arâmil: Father of Widows
343	Wahîd: Unique One.	344	Sayyid: Master.
345	Jâmi`: Unifier.	346	Muqtafi: Imitated One.
347	Kâmil: Perfect One.	348	afi Allah: Allah's Chosen and Purified One.?340. Naji Allah: Allah's Intimate Friend.
349	Kalîm Allah: Conversant With Allah.	350	Muhyin: Giver of Life.
351	Munajji: Savior.	352	Ma`lum: Of Known Position.
353	Shahîr: Famous.	354	Mashhud: Visible.
355	Misbâh: Lamp.	356	Mad`uw: Called upon?
357	Mujib: Responsive to Requests.	358	Mujab: Whose Request is Granted.
359	Hafiy: Affectionate and Kind.	360	Mukarram: Highly Honored.
361	Matîn: Steadfast.	362	Mu'ammil: Rouser of Hope
363	Wasûl: Conveyer	364	Dhu hurma: Sacrosanct.

365	Dhu makâna: Of Eminent Station.	366	Dhu 'izz: Endowed With Might.
367	Dhu Fadl: Pre-Eminent.	368	Ghawth: Helper.
369	Ghayyath: Prompt and Frequent Helper.	370	Hadiyyatullah: Allah's Gift.
371	Sirât Allah: The Way to Allah.	372	Dhikrullah: The Remembrance of Allah.
373	Hizbullah: The Party of Allah.	374	Muntaqa: Carefully Selected.
375	Abu al-Tahir: Father of Tahir	376	Barr: Pious. Dutiful.
377	Mubirr: Who Overcomes.	378	Wajîh: Distinguished In Allah's Sight.
379	Nasîh: One Who Excels At Sincere Advice.	380	Wakîl: Trustee. Dependable.
381	Kafîl: Guarantor. Guardian.	382	Shafîq: Solicitous. Tender.
383	Ruh al-qist: The Spirit of Justice.	384	Muktafi: Does With Little.
385	Bâligh: One Who Has Reached His Goal?	386	Shâfi: Healer.
387	Wâsil: One Who has Reached His Goal.	388	Mawsûl: Connected.
389	Sâ'iq: (Mindful) Conductor.	390	Muhdi: Guide.
391	Muqaddam: Pre-eminent One.	392	Fâdil: Most Excellent One.
393	Miftâh: Key.	394	Miftâh al-rahma: The Key to Mercy.
395	Miftâh al-janna: The Key to Paradise.	396	'Alam al-iman: The Standard of Belief.
397	'Alam al-yaqîn: The Standard of Certainty.	398	Dalîl al-khayrât: The Guide to Good Things.
399	Musahhih al-hasanât: The Ratifier of Good Deeds.	400	Muqîl al-'atharât: The Dismisser of Private Faults.
401	Safûh 'an al-zallât: The One Who Disregards Lapses.	402	Sâhib al-qadam: Possessor of The Foothold.
403	Makhsûs bi al-'izz: Alone to Be Granted Might.	404	Makhsûs bi al-majd: Alone to Be Granted Glory.
405	Makhsûs bi al-sharaf: Alone to Be Granted Honor.	406	Sâhib al-fadîla: Possessor of Greatest Pre-Eminence.

407	Sâhib al-izâr: The Wearer of the Loin-wrap.	408	Sâhib al-rida': The Wearer of the Cloak.
409	Sâhib al-daraja al-rafî'a: Possessor of the Highest Degree.	410	Sâhib al-mighfar: Possessor of the Helmet.?
411	Sâhib al-bayân: The Spokesman.	412	Mutahhar al-janân: Purified of Heart.
413	Sahîh al-islam: Completer of Islam.	414	Sayyid al-kawnayn: Master of Humanity and Jinn.
415	'Ayn al-na'îm: Spring of Bliss. Bliss Itself.	416	'Ayn al-ghurr: Spring of the Radiant Ones. Radiance Itself.
417	Sa'dullah: Felicity Bestowed by Allah.	418	Sa'd al-khalq: Felicited Bestowed Upon Creation.
419	Khatîb al-umam: The Orator to the Nations.	420	'Alam al-huda: Flag of Guidance.
421	Kâshif al-kurab: Remover of Adversities.	422	Râfi' al-rutab: The Raiser of Ranks.
423	'Izz al-'arab: Might and Glory of the Arabs.	424	Sâhib al-faraj: Bringer of Deliverance.

Defining the Unknowable Allah

Having presented the boundaries and restrictions of the exposition of and the three categories of the Doctrine of Allah (Tawheed), we now turn our attention to consider other aspects of this doctrine, bearing in mind the fact that Allah is unknowable.

Genderless Allah?

Speaking of the use of the word "he" to address Allah, since "he" is "genderless", the use of the word "he" is an anomaly—but perhaps an inevitable and necessary one—because, although "he" is genderless, it would not be appropriate to call a deity "it". This is an issue within the context of the Arabic language in regard to gender, as Arabic does not have an "it", but only masculine and feminine. However, even within Islam, since the very idea of any hint of "self revelation" by Allah is "Kufr", this leaves "him" even more of a mystery right from the start.

One Allah? What Does that Mean?

In the Appendix we provide a comprehensive listing of the occurrences of the word "one" and its variations in the Arabic language as it relates to the coinage of the word "Tawheed." These are:

1. "wahed" (وَاحِد)
2. "al-wahed" (أَلْوَاحِدُ)
3. "wahedan" (وَاحِداً)
4. "ahad" (أَحَدٌ)
5. "No deity except 'he'" (لا إِلَـهَ إِلاَّ هُو)

Neither the Qur'an nor the Hadith explains the meaning of this term "one", since *"there is none like him."* Therefore, is he:

a) One in number, mathematically?
b) One of a kind?
c) One in substance?
d) One in form?
e) One shape or colour?
f) One in gender?
g) One in spirit?

The "one in spirit" is especially problematic since even Muhammad was not informed sufficiently about the spirit as per Surah 17:85, *"And they ask you (O Muhammad) concerning the ruh (the spirit); say: 'The ruh (the spirit): it is one of the things, the knowledge of which is only with my Lord. And of knowledge, you have been given only a little.'"*

However, the main emphasis in the Qur'an, the Hadith, and the entirety of Islamic scholarship is that Allah is "one, with no partners."

Is Anything Impossible with Allah?

The linkage of the two central assertions of the Doctrines of Tawheed (absolute oneness of Allah) and Tanzeeh (absolute lack of any resemblance or incarnation) would produce a significant internal inconsistency. On the one hand, Islam would assert that Allah's power and authority is absolute and limitless, but because of the combined Tawheed and Tanzeeh doctrines, one ends up with what can be called the Islamic concept of the "impossibilities" or the "limitations" of Allah.

The question arises, how is it possible that the Allah of Islam could have any limitations whatsoever? Are there things that are impossible for him to do? Just how free is he, or how limited is he?

At this juncture, once more the implications of Surah 42:11, that *"There is nothing like him…"* raises a new question. According to Islam, Allah cannot cross over his realm in the other world to man's world for any reason. He cannot be seen by mankind as he remains invisible in the other world. As a consequence, nothing is made in his image, nor can it be. Because of this boundary limitation, he can never be incarnate, nor can he ever be a Father. Fatherhood is seen as a human product. It would diminish Allah's authority by humanizing him.

He is limited further (both spatially and relationally) in regard to speaking directly to mankind—because as indicated above, he cannot enter man's realm.

But there is yet another constraint which would apply even if he were not bound within his own realm. This is a limitation of propriety; as the Qur'an says it "isn't fitting" that he should speak directly to a man, face-to-face, person-to-person:

> *"It is not fitting for a man that Allah should speak to him except by inspiration, or from behind a veil, or by the sending of a messenger to reveal, with Allah's permission, what Allah wills …"* Surah 42:51.

Since "it isn't fitting" that Allah could or would speak directly to a man, according to Surah 42:51, he could neither make a promise nor a covenant with man or mankind, or with their representative. Thus we can safely point out that Allah did not walk, talk, or have fellowship with Adam in the Garden, nor did he later speak directly to Ibrahim, Is-haq, or Yaqoub. The two exceptions in the Qur'an which give the distinct appearance of a relationship are: (1) Muslim prophet Ibrahim who is said to be "Khalil Allah"[75] (i.e. Allah's friend) and (2) Muslim prophet Moosa, who is said to be "Kaleem Allah"[76] (i.e. The one to whom Allah spoke). However, it is

---

75 Surah 4:125, " ….And Allah did take Ibrahim (Abraham) as a *Khalil* (a friend)", i.e. within the context of being loyal to Muslims with enmity to non-Muslims (Doctrine of Al-Walaa' wal Baraa'). See the Tafsir by Tabari: http://www.altafsir.com/Tafasir.asp?tMadhNo=1&tTafsirNo=1&t-SoraNo=4&tAyahNo=125&tDisplay=yes&UserProfile=0&LanguageId=1

76 Surah 4:164, "…and to Moosa (Moses) Allah spoke directly (Takleem in Arabic)," i.e. Moosa received a particular Wahy called Takleem, hence Allah did not speak to him directly or face to face. Tafsir scholars would state that this kind of Wahy was given also to Muhammad who received more Wahy than all the prophets and messengers combined. In other words this is nothing but a smoke-screen and another carefully crafted illusion.

explained in the commentaries that in these exceptions, Allah never revealed anything personal about himself.

Furthermore, even if it were "fitting" to speak directly to a prophet, Allah could not *conclude* a covenant by which he would be bound, for yet another reason.

This is because of his absolute authority. If Allah were to commit or bind himself in a covenant relationship—either conditional or unconditional— he would in a very real sense be constrained, or "limited", whereas he is totally unaccountable.

Allah, being who he is, is unlimited in power and is absolute in his authority. This means he is absolutely unlimited in all his prerogatives.

Prohibition of Sensitive "Questioning"

So, Islamically speaking, the logical question one might want to ask would be, "Given that Allah is absolute in power and unlimited in prerogatives, what would stop him from overruling the spatial and the propriety limitations?" However, this question is not only unanswerable, it raises yet another question by entering into the realm of "forbidden questions."

Not only is there no answer, one is even prohibited from asking the question—as this would be entering a domain to which no one is allowed access:

> "*O ye who have believed, do not ask about things which if made plain to you will trouble you...*" Surah 5:101

Thus, as confirmed in the following Surah, Allah can *never ever* be questioned:

> "*He cannot be questioned as to what he does ...*" (Surah 21:23)

So, even the question raised at the outset of this section, "Why is Allah called 'he', when he is genderless?", will fall into the domain of forbidden questions as "Allah knows best." This expression, "Allah knows best", is used by all Islamic scholars at the end of a fatwa or dissertation to indicate their limitations in whatever opinion they had advanced.

Allah's "Relationship" to his Creation

Clearly, Allah is non-relational in all aspects, unless one considers the role of master and slave a sufficient relationship. However, even a slave knows his master, whether he is harsh or kind. But in Islam nobody knows this Allah. Not withstanding this dilemma, some Muslims claim that they have a relationship with him. But, based on other foundational Islamic doctrines, it can be clearly deduced that such claims are illusions or wishful thinking. In the Qur'an, the sole purpose of the creation of man was to be Allah's slave:

- (Surah 2:186), "...*if my servants or my slaves ask you about me...*",

- (Surah 14:31) "...*command my slaves to establish regular prayers..*"

- (Surah 15:42), saying to Satan "*Certainly, you shall have no authority over my slaves...*"

So, although Allah is not known or knowable in any intimate or personal way, he is accepted always as a "Master". This "master", having unlimited prerogatives, is to be obeyed, and is to be obeyed unilaterally. And if loved by his slaves, that would be unilateral also.

Therefore, we do not know him, nor can we know him. We cannot even know his character through his attributes and 99 names. He is, by definition, incomparable.

For instance, let us take the attribute "Merciful". His mercy, his compassion, his forgiveness, etc., are all based on the central assumption "*... there is nothing like him...*". Although positive sounding, and perhaps very comforting to the individual Muslim, in the end these are empty or void terms, for he and his attributes cannot be understood or perceived because—again we hit the same dead-end, "*... there is nothing like him ...*".

Since the mercy of man is not like the mercy of Allah, to compare or contrast the mercy of Allah to that of the mercy of a man would be to humanize or anthropomorphize him. In turn, such a humanization of Allah is ultimate "Kufr" (blasphemy)—for again, "*... there is nothing like him...*" in shape, form, or character.

Yet, after laboring over the need NOT to humanize Allah or to divinize a man, the Qur'an singles out Muhammad, a mere man, to be the embodiment of the mercies of Allah, and has been further equated with the quality of "mercy" equivalent to that of Allah by a Qur'anic injunction according to Surah 21:107:

"And we have sent you (O Muhammad) not but as a mercy for all the worlds (Angels, Jinn and humans)."[77]

as well as, Surah 9:128

"There has come unto you a messenger (Muhammad) from amongst your-selves. It grieves him that you should receive any injury or difficulty. He is anxious over you, for the believers, he is full of pity, kind, and merciful."

Allah is Confined to His Own Realm

So we see that the Allah of the Qur'an is bound within his own realm and within Qur'anic protocols whereby there is no personal contact whatsoever in the here and now, or in eternity. Insofar as to his person and essence, he is eternally unknown, and unknowable, but he only declared his will and his directives for the "worlds" to his chosen and final prophet Muhammad through the angel Jibril (Gabriel).

Although Allah does not reveal himself, he makes demands by laying down rules—rights and wrongs—with no clear consistencies. As these rules are relative, Allah wants to "lighten the burden of his slaves." And as he changes his standard and his revelations there are no absolutes with Allah. Hence, all is relative according to the following:

- Surah 2:286, *"Allah burdens not a person beyond his scope...."*
- Surah 64:16, *"So keep your duty to Allah and fear Him as much as you can..."*

Allah's "Creation" and the Implications Thereof

First of all, we have seen that the Qur'anic creation account of Adam is at best contradictory and confusing. Was Adam created from a congealed clot of blood (Surah 96:2), from "sounding clay" (Surah 15:26), from a sperm (Surah 23:13, 16:4), from water (Surah 25:54), or from dust (Surah 22:5, 3:59)? It is unclear.

---

77 Interestingly, the Allah of Islam declares in the Qur'an that Muhammad is ruthless toward the unbelievers as in Surah 48:29, *"Muhammad is an apostle of Allah, him and those that are with him are ruthless on the unbelievers"*. Furthermore, Allah commands Muhammad *"...to incite and entice the believers to kill for the cause of Allah...* (Surah 8:65) *"beheading them, subduing them, raising ransom..."* (Surah 47:4)

But most importantly, Adam was NOT created in God's image as per Genesis 1:26, as the Allah of the Qur'an is unknowable, and since *"...there is nothing like unto him ..."*, he remains "imageless". Hence, to say that Adam was created in the likeness or image of Allah is Kufr (blasphemy).

In the Qur'an, there is no Fall, i.e. "original sin", hence there is no need for redemption. Accordingly *"...man was created weak ..."* (Surah 4:28), *"forgetful"* (Surah 20:110) and created into *"...toil and struggle..."* (Surah 90:4).

Therefore, Islam denies man's inherent sin nature as a consequence of the Fall, and hence the need for a savior. Instead it establishes mankind's Islamic identity in the "Fitrah Doctrine" which declares that the nature of "man" is Islam (Surah 30:30), as is based on an imposed covenant by Allah toward the descendants of Adam (Surah 7:172). In this imposed covenant, Allah extracts a promise from Adam and all his descendants to be Muslims, and promises only punishment for disobedience. All non-Muslims are automatically disobedient and as a result, in violation of this covenant—hence the constitutional inferiority of all non-Muslims.

Jinns among the Creation?

Also, Allah's "creation" refers to strange beings called, Jinn. The Jinn are in the world, invisible, unseen, yet living with mankind closely and in association with them. This close association of humans and Jinn is manifested in the declared purpose of Allah's creation,

> *"I (Allah) have created the Jinn and Uns (humankind) only to serve me."* (Surah 51:56).

They are capable of being Muslims or Kafirs (unbelievers): Surah 46:29[78] and Surah 72:1-15[79].

---

78 Surah 46:29, *"And when we sent towards you (Muhammad)several persons of the jinn, listening to the Qur'an, when they stood in the presence thereof, they said: 'Listen in silence' And when it was finished, they returned to their people, as warners."*

79 Surah 72:1-15, *"Say: It has been revealed to me that a **company of Jinns** listened (to the Qur'an). They said, 'We have really heard a wonderful recital. 'It gives guidance to the right, and we have believed therein: we shall not join any other gods with our Lord. And exalted is the majesty of our Lord: He has taken neither a wife nor a son. **There were some foolish ones among us, who used to utter extravagant lies against Allah;** but we do think that no man or spirit should say aught that untrue against Allah. True, there were persons among mankind who took shelter with persons among the Jinns, but they increased them in folly. And they think as you thought, that Allah would not raise up any one (to judgment). And we pried into the secrets of heaven; but we found it filled with stern guards and flaming fires. We used, indeed, to sit there in stations, to a hearing; but any who listen now will find a flaming fire watching him in ambush. And we understand not*

Regarding these Jinn, most non-Muslim scholars insist that the belief in Jinn is "folk Islam." In reality, the doctrine of the Jinn is a core doctrine of Islam. It affects all Islamic beliefs from creation to its eschatological doctrines. Thus it affects Muslims individually and collectively from birth to death—as to how they view their identity, barrenness, daily provisions, and all other religious aspects of their lives.

The Qur'an is saturated with references to Jinn, and Muhammad was the only prophet who was uniquely sent to both Jinn and humankind.

The "Love" of Allah and Love of Neighbor?

At the center of Biblical Christianity is the theme throughout that *"God is Love."* (1 John 4:8). This is manifested by creating man in His image, in His promise of salvation, His covenants, and the fulfillment of His promises through the sacrifice of His son on the cross. The story of the prodigal son is a profound parable, which illustrates the depth of the love of the LORD God (Luke 15:11-32).

Jesus Christ Himself would declare that the two greatest commandments are: Love of God and love of neighbor (Matthew 22:36-40).

In the "Come to a Common Word between Us and You" letter by 138 Muslim scholars to the "Church"[80], they would posit that the "Love of God and Love of Neighbor" form the "common ground" between Muslims and Christians. But is that really the case?

As outlined in [Ref. 4][81] the author's response to this "Common Word" initiative, we argue that the "love of God and love of neighbor" is an illusion. For Islam teaches a different doctrine, the doctrine of "Al-Walaa' wal-Baraa'" (Allegiance and Rejection). We quote from this reference the following state-

---

*whether ill is intended to those on earth, or whether their Lord intends to guide them to right conduct. There are among us some that are righteous, and some the contrary: we follow divergent paths. But we think that we can by no means frustrate Allah throughout the earth, nor can we frustrate him by flight. And as for us, since we have listened to the guidance (Qur'an), we have accepted it (i.e. became Muslims): and any who believes in his Lord has no fear, either of a short (account) or of any injustice. **Amongst us are some that submit their wills, and some that swerve from justice.** Now those who submit their wills - they have sought out the right conduct (Islam): But those who swerve,- they are fuel for hell-fire."*

80 http://www.acommonword.com/the-acw-document/
81 Sam Solomon and E. Al Maqdisi, ***The Common Word: The Undermining of the Church***, www.pilcrowpress.com

ment from a modern moderate Muslim scholar who bases all his arguments on irrefutable Islamic manuals:

> "Dr. Abdel Rehman Abdel Khaliq sums up the Islamic position accurately ... when he says: 'the only business of a Muslim is to humiliate the kafir (non-believer) and make him surrender or to Islamize him thus preventing a greater corruption by undertaking a lesser one. For the reality and the root of the relationship between a Muslim and a non-Muslim is enmity and war, Surah's 8:39, 9:29, and 58:22.'"

- Surah 8:39, "*And fight them until there is no fitnah (disbelief) and the religion, all of it, is for Allah. And if they cease - then indeed, Allah is seeing of what they do.*"

- Surah 9:29, "*Fight those who do not believe in Allah or in the last day and who do not consider unlawful what Allah and his messenger have made unlawful and who do not adopt the religion of truth from those who were given the scripture - fight until they give the jizyah (punishment tax) willingly while they are humbled.*"

- Surah 58:22, "*You will not find a people who believe in Allah and the last day having affection for those who oppose Allah and his messenger, even if they were their fathers or their sons or their brothers or their kindred. ...*".

Yet, the "common word" letter by the 138 Muslim scholars would quote a weak Hadith, "*None of you has faith until you love for your neighbor what you love for yourself.*"[80]

But as explained in [Ref. 4] this "love" must be *by Muslims to other Muslims* in accordance with the doctrine of Allegiance and Rejection (Al-Walaa' wal-Baraa').

Beyond that, Muslims cannot "love" Allah except by following Muhammad, according to:

- Surah 4:80, "*Whosoever obeys the messenger, has already obeyed Allah ...*"

- Surah 33:6, "*The Prophet is closer/dearer to the believers than their own souls ...*"

- Surah 3:31, "*Say, (O Muhammad), 'If you should love Allah, then follow me, so that Allah will love you and forgive you your sins...'*"

- Surah 49:3, *"Indeed, those who lower their voices before the messenger of Allah - they are the ones whose hearts Allah has tested for righteousness. For them is forgiveness and great reward."*

Interestingly, the only name/attribute of Allah that resembles the idea of love is "Al-Wadud" (The kind or affectionate one).

According to the understanding of Muslim scholars and commentators of the Qur'an they all agree that the affections of Allah are expressed through his messenger Muhammad. The affection of the Muslims for Muhammad is an absolute requirement by divine decree.[82]

This concept of Al-Wadud is an abstract notion. It is not based on any covenant relationship, neither it is promulgated on Allah's side. But it is commanded and it is for the Muslims to fulfill it by their obedience.

So once again there is no resemblance or any form of similarity between Allah's affection (i.e. Wudud) as recorded in the Qur'an in Surah's 85:14 and 11:90,

- Surah 85:14, *"And he is (Al-Wadud) the forgiving, the affectionate"*,

- Surah 11:90, *"And ask forgiveness of your Lord and then repent to him. Indeed, my Lord is (Wadud) merciful and affectionate"*,

and the Biblical love of God which is demonstrated through the sacrifice of His one and only begotten Son, Jesus Christ. It is His love towards us and not ours towards him.

Degeneration of the Doctrine of Allah into the Finality of Muhammad

Given the Divergence, Where do We Go from Here?

From the foregoing we have discovered that in no way can the LORD God of the Bible be the same as the Allah of Islam. The Biblical narrative that Islam attempted to circumvent by building a related but alternative one, is built on the LORD God's *positive* revelation. The LORD God revealed Himself in so many ways; as the book of Hebrews summarizes it, *"¹ In the past God spoke to*

---

[82] The following fatwa is given in the Appendix to substantiates that the love of Muhammad is a divine decree issued by Allah to be fulfilled by all Muslims https://islamqa.info/en/14250

our ancestors through the prophets at many times and in various ways, ² *but in these last days he has spoken to us by his Son, whom he appointed heir of all things, and through whom also he made the universe."* (Heb. 1:1-2) The LORD God created man in His image (Gen. 1:26-27), recognized Adam's "sin" and provided a roadmap for salvation through the "seed of the woman" (Gen. 3:15).

The LORD God of the Judeo-Christian scriptures not only has revealed Himself, but has persisted in His love and compassion toward His creatures—binding and securing this relationship through a series of covenants. The Biblical narrative is punctuated by eight *covenants.* The (1) Edenic, (2) Adamic (3) Noahic, (4) Abrahamic (5) Land, (6) Mosaic, (7) Davidic, and (8) New Covenants. These covenants enabled His people to approach Him and access Him. He heard and answered their pleas. In other words, He is knowable, relational and compassionate despite their failures and shortfalls. Amazingly, out of the eight covenants, only two are conditional or bilateral. The rest are unconditional and unilateral from His side.

The LORD God "Tabernacled" with us, *"For the law was given through Moses; grace and truth came through Jesus Christ."* (John 1:17). He came to us in the flesh as God Incarnate, *"The Word became flesh and made his dwelling among us. We have seen his glory, the glory of the one and only Son, who came from the Father, full of grace and truth."* (John 1:14). The LORD God not only made Himself known, but wants every human being to know Him, whereby He, *"... desires all men to be saved and to come to the knowledge of the truth.."* (1 Tim. 2:4)

In contrast, and as elaborated upon in detail earlier, the Allah of Islam is described only in negative terms, *"... there is none like unto him ..."* (Surah 42:11), he is unrelated to his creation, *"¹·Say (O Muhammad): 'He is Allah, (the) one. ²·The self-sufficient master. ³·He begets not, nor was he begotten; ⁴·And there is none co-equal or comparable unto him'"* (Surah 112). Allah does not commit himself to any covenants. Instead he imposes that mankind is created to submit to him (Surah 7:172) and to serve him. Not only is he unrecognizable, he is completely "unknowable." Yet the Islamic counter narrative to the Biblical one claims that Tawheed is the true and original monotheism, that all the "Biblical" characters are Muslim, and that the Bible itself emanated from the same source as the Qur'an.

In the final analysis, based on the foregoing, how can anyone ever know anything about Allah? And to say that he could be known, or that he is incarnate in Jesus Christ, and that he indwells believers is the pinnacle of Shirk.

Yet Muslim scholars have struggled to provide information on Allah, only to always fall back to the position of the four boundaries, which are all negative, but holding on to the line that Allah's words have to be accepted at face value as given in the Qur'an, as "Allah knows best."

In what follows, we provide some commentaries on the "official" doctrine of Allah, which by its internal logic and the words of the Qur'an collapses into what we may conclude as the "doctrine of the Finality of Muhammad"!

Finality of Muhammad

Further to the details of the three-pronged classification associated with the doctrine of Allah, one is reminded of the following issues which were discussed earlier:

1. All the prophets were Muslims, preached Islam and spoke of Muhammad, with special reference to the so-called "Anchor Prophets", i.e. Ulul-Azm, in Arabic. (See Figure 9 on the following page, and also Surah 3:81 stated earlier)

2. The Qur'an is the last and final set of instructions to mankind, and Muhammad, the final and the last prophet, is the most favored with Allah and is the perfect man, the exemplar, whom mankind has been instructed to follow and emulate. He is the perfect model by Allah's command, as revealed in the Qur'an and the Sunnah—so much so, that amongst some of his titles are: master of creation and creatures, seal of all the prophets, lord of all the prophets, light of Allah. As such, he is in absolute charge over mankind and their affairs, jointly with Allah.

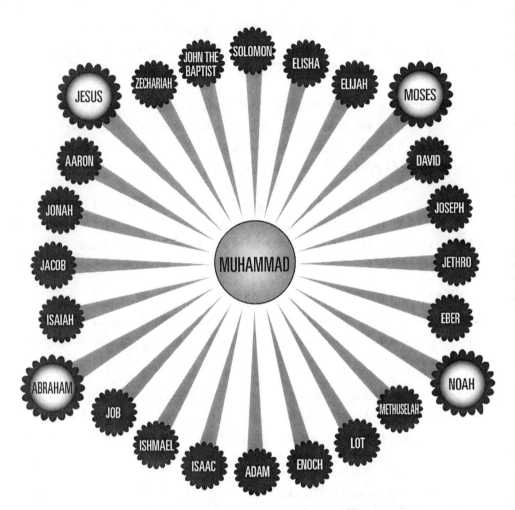

Figure 9: In this abstract figure (based on the Islamic tree of the prophets), we illustrate the central Islamic theme that not only all the prophets were Muslims, but also they were bound by a pact from Allah to believe in Muhammad, to serve him and aid him in victory according to Surah 3:81

Hence there is nothing and no part of Islam that can be understood or handled without Muhammad, be it Islamic beliefs, Islamic practices, Islamic doctrines, Islamic Shariah, Islamic conduct, Islamic dress codes, Islamic diet—and much more. Although the three categories of Tawheed and their classification, which we explained and which are supposed to be only about Allah, Muhammad remains not only an integral part of it, but remains inseparable and central to it.

Interestingly, this tight association between Muhammad and Allah might sound like Shirk (i.e. making partners with Allah) and may well be so by the Islamic definition itself. The authoritative Muslim Scholar Ibn Taymiyyah said[83]:

> *"The declaration of faith, 'There is no god but Allah', requires you to love only for the sake of Allah, to hate only for the sake of Allah, to ally yourself only for the sake of Allah, to declare enmity only for the sake of Allah; it requires you to love what Allah loves and to hate what Allah hates. It also requires you to ally yourself to the Muslims wherever you find them and to oppose the disbelievers even if they are your closest kin."*

Based on what every ancient and modern Muslim scholar without exception has said and written, Allah and his "messenger" Muhammad, are inseparable, and no distinction can be made between them. This is posited and articulated by Ibn Tayymiah:[84]

> *"Allah's rights and the messenger's rights are equal and same. The sanctity of Allah is the same as that of Muhammad. Whoever vexes the messenger vexes Allah, and whoever obeys the messenger then he has already obeyed Allah, because the 'Ummah' has no connection with their creator except through the messenger. No one has a means to Allah except through the Messenger, and Allah has substituted Muhammad for himself in all matters for commanding and forbidding, and revealing. No distinction is allowed to be made between Allah and his messenger in any of these matters."*

Qur'anic Injunctions of Muhammad's Finality and Their Implications

Having discovered the finality of Muhammad from the necessity of the Shahadah, his names, the need to obey him in order to obey Allah and much more, the following is a limited list of Qur'anic injunctions on this subject.

These are grouped into seven categories:

1. Obedience/disobedience to Allah through Muhammad and the resulting rewards/punishments.

2. Whatever belongs to Allah belongs to Muhammad.

---

83 Ibn Taymiyyah, *Al-Ihtijaj bi'l- Qadar,* page 62.
84 Ibn Taymiyyah, *Assarim al Maslool ala Shatim Arrasoul*, in pages 40-41. This landmark book details the full scope of the Islamic law to severely punish anyone or any entity for the slightest criticism of Muhammad.

3. Allah's favor for the sake of Muhammad.

4. Allah doing his best to please Muhammad.

5. Allah & Muhammad as co-legislators.

6. Allah's terror towards those who disobey Muhammad.

7. Total Inseparability between Allah and Muhammad.

1. Obedience/disobedience to Allah through Muhammad and the resulting rewards/punishments

The general principle here is that since Allah's purpose in creating Jinns and humankind is to serve him, in a master/slave relationship according to the Worship Tawheed (Tawheed Al-Uluhiyyah), the knowledge of which came through what Allah communicated via Jibril/Wahy process to Muhammad. Such servitude by Jinns and humans is attainable by means of "obedience." But this obedience to the unknowable Allah is attainable only by obeying Muhammad. Obedience has its rewards and disobedience, its punishments.

In the Surah's below we have inserted explanatory comments.

- Surah 4:80, "*He who obeys the messenger (Muhammad), has indeed obeyed Allah….*" (Obedience to Muhammad is pre-requisite to obedience to Allah.)

- Surah 3:32, "*Say (O Muhammad): 'Obey Allah and the messenger (Muhammad).' But if they turn away, then Allah does not like the disbelievers.*" (Allah's "love" is reserved only to believers.)

- Surah 3:132, "*And obey Allah and the messenger (Muhammad) that you may obtain mercy.*" (Mercy (not grace) is the result of obedience to Allah and Muhammad.)

- Surah 4:13, "*… and whosoever disobeys Allah and his messenger (Muhammad), and transgresses His limits, He will cast him into the Fire, to abide therein; and he shall have a disgraceful torment.*" (Disobedience leads to hell fire.)

- Surah 4:14, "*And whosoever disobeys Allah and his messenger (Muhammad), and transgresses His limits, He will cast him into the Fire, to abide therein; and he shall have a disgraceful torment.*" (Disobedience leads to hell fire.)

- Surah 4:59, *"O you who believe!* **Obey Allah and obey the messenger** *(Muhammad), and those of you (Muslims) who are in authority. (And) if you differ in anything amongst yourselves,* **refer it to Allah and his messenger,** *if you believe in Allah and in the last day. That is better and more suitable for final determination."* (Obedience, taking counsel, and belief in Allah and the last day are commanded, so that final authority resides in both Allah and Muhammad.)

- Surah 4:64, *"We sent no messenger, but to be obeyed by Allah's leave. If they (hypocrites), when they had been unjust to themselves, had come to you (Muhammad) and begged Allah's forgiveness, and the* **messenger had begged forgiveness for them:** *indeed, they would have found Allah all-forgiving, most merciful."* (Muhammad's intercession leads to Allah's forgiveness.)

- Surah 8:46, *"And* **obey Allah and his messenger,** *and do not dispute (with one another) lest you lose courage and your strength depart, and be patient...."* (Obedience and ending disputes provides strength and patience.)

- Surah 9:71, *"And the believers, both men and women, are allies of one another ... and they* **obey Allah and his messenger.** *..."* (Linking of obedience to the unity of the Muslim Ummah is established in the doctrine of Al-Walaa' wal Baraa' [Allegiance to Muslims and enmity to non-Muslims].)

- Surah 24:50, *"Is there a disease in their hearts? Or do they doubt or fear lest* **Allah and his messenger** *should wrong them in judgment...?"*

- Surah 33:71, *"He will direct you to do righteous good deeds and will forgive you your sins. And* **whosoever obeys Allah and his messenger** *has indeed achieved a great achievement (i.e. he will be saved from the Hell-fire and made to enter Paradise)."*

- Surah 4:69, *"Whoever* **obeys Allah and the messenger,** *they are with those whom Allah has blessed of the prophets and the truthful, and the martyrs, and the righteous. What fine companions they are!!"* (Obedience leads to companionship with the martyrs, prophets and the righteous.)

- Surah 5:92, *"And* **obey Allah and obey the messenger,** *and beware; but if you turn away, then know that Our Messenger's duty is only to pro-*

claim plainly." (Obedience to Muhammad and Allah as conveyed through Muhammad.)

- Surah 8:12-13, "12 *When your Lord inspired the angels, (saying), 'I am with you, so make the believers stand-firm. I shall cast terror into the hearts of the disbelievers; so smite above the necks, and smite of them every finger. 13 This is because they* **contended against Allah and his messenger.** *And whoever contends against Allah and his messenger, then, Allah is severe in punishment.*" (Disobedience leads to severe punishment.)

2. Whatever belongs to Allah belongs to Muhammad

- Surah 8:1, "*They ask you (O Muhammad) about the spoils of war. Say:* **'The spoils are for Allah and the messenger.'** *So fear Allah and adjust all matters of difference among you, and obey Allah and his messenger (Muhammad), if you are believers.*" (Spoils of war are jointly owned by Allah and Muhammad.)

- Surah 8:41, "*And know that whatever of war-booty that you may gain,* **one fifth (1/5th) of it is assigned to Allah, and to the messenger,** *and to the near relatives(of Muhammad), the orphans, the poor, and the wayfarer, if you have believed in Allah and in that which we sent down to our slave (Muhammad) on the day of criterion, the day when the two armies met - And Allah is able to do all things.*" (This Surah provides the principle of disbursement of the war booty.)

- Surah 9:59, "*Would that they were contented with what Allah and his messenger gave them and had said: 'Allah is Sufficient for us.* **Allah will give us of his bounty, together with his messenger...**'"

- Surah 59:7, "*That which Allah gives as spoil unto his messenger from the people of the townships, it is for Allah and his messenger and for the near of kin and the orphans and the needy and the wayfarer, that it become not a commodity between the rich among you. And whatsoever the messenger gives you, take it. And whatsoever he forbids, abstain (from it). And keep your duty to Allah. Allah is stern in reprisal.*" (This verse abrogates the previous two. As stated in the above (Surah 8:41) Muhammad limited his and Allah's portion of the war booty to one fifth. But now, he would declare that Allah has given him authority to keep whatever he wishes and to disperse it to whomever he chooses.)

- Surah 33:22, "*And when the believers saw the confederates, they said: 'This is what Allah and his Messenger had promised us, and Allah and his messenger had spoken the truth, and it only added to their faith and to their submissiveness.'*" (This speaks of the parity between Allah and Muhammad.)

- Surah 33.29, "*But if you desire Allah and his messenger, and the home of the hereafter, then Allah has prepared for good-doers amongst you an enormous reward.*" (This is related to the unequal treatment of his wives.)

- Surah 8:24, "*O you who believe. Answer Allah and his messenger when he (Muhammad) calls you ...*" (This also speaks of the parity between Allah and Muhammad.)

3. Allah's Favor for the Sake of Muhammad

Although Allah is unknowable and in another realm, he has favored Muhammad uniquely. Aside from requiring obedience to Muhammad to achieve his purposes, Allah shows various forms of favor and "kindness" to Muhammad. But since one cannot discuss "how" these favors are accomplished, it must be left at face value according to the following Qur'anic directives:

- Surah 3:31, "*Say (O Muhammad to mankind): 'If you love Allah then follow me, Allah will love you and forgive you of your sins. And Allah is oft-forgiving, most merciful.'*" (The "love" of Allah starts by following Muhammad.)

- Surah 3:132, "*And obey Allah and the messenger that you may obtain mercy.*" (The result of obedience to Muhammad is Allah's "mercy". Note that Allah's mercy cannot be explained in human terms. Allah alone knows that.)

- Surah 57:28, "*O you who believe, fear Allah and believe in his messenger, and he will give you a twofold portion of his mercy; and he will assign for you a light by which you will walk and forgive you; for Allah is forgiving, merciful.*" (Jews and Christians are given double rewards if they fear Allah and believe in Muhammad.)

4. Allah Doing his Best to Please Muhammad

The favors of Allah are now translated into responding to Muhammad's feelings, especially after some encounters or setbacks. Furthermore, Muhammad is given special privileges not given to anyone, like having an unlimited number of wives. Muhammad is to be greeted in the best manner, his wives are to be hidden behind a veil, and those who mock him are to be severely punished.

- Surah 93:5, "*And your Lord will give you so that you shall be well-pleased.*"

- Surah 2:144, "*We have seen the turning of your face towards the heaven. Surely, we shall turn you to a Qiblah (prayer direction) **that shall please you...**"* (The pleasing concept of both 93:5 and 2:144 and others, illustrates Allah exerting the effort to please his messenger Muhammad. Note that the implications of 2:144 establishes major rituals of Islam and the sanctities of Mecca for the sake of Muhammad and his appeasement by Allah.)

- Surah 33:50 – 51, "*50 O Prophet, we have made lawful to you your wives, to whom you have paid their bridal money, and those whom your right hand possesses - ... 51 You (O Muhammad) can postpone (the turn of) whom you will of them (your wives), and you may receive whom you will...*" (In this crucial verse, Allah would give Muhammad unique privileges not given to anyone, including the marrying of an unlimited number of women.)

- Surah 33:53, "*O you who believe! Enter not the Prophet's houses, except when leave is given to you for a meal, (and then) not (so early as) to wait for its preparation. But when you are invited, enter, and when you have taken your meal, disperse, without sitting for a talk. **Suchactivity annoys the prophet, and he is shy of asking you to go, but Allah is not shy of telling you the truth.** And when you ask (his wives) for anything you want, ask them from behind a screen, that is purer for your hearts and for their hearts. And it is not for **you that you should annoy Allah's messenger,** nor that you should ever marry his wives after him. With Allah that shall be an enormity.*" (Allah is commanding the Muslims not to annoy the prophet, that his women should be seen only behind a veil, and much more.)

- Surah 49:1, "*O you who believe: **Do not put yourselves forward before Allah and his messenger, and fear Allah...**"* (This is a call from Allah to Muslims that they show full respect to Muhammad.)

- Surah 49:2-4, "*2 O you who believe! **Raise not your voices above the voice of the prophet**, nor speak aloud to him in talk as you speak aloud to one another, lest your deeds may be rendered fruitless while you perceive not. 3 Those who lower their voices in the presence of Allah's messenger, **they are the ones whose hearts Allah has tested for piety**. For them is forgiveness and a great reward. 4 **Those who call you from behind the dwellings, most of them have no sense**.*" (Again Allah is commanding a reverence for Muhammad, and is forbidding opposition to him in any form or shape.)

- Surah 58:8, "*Have you not seen those who were forbidden to hold secret counsels, and afterwards returned to that which they had been forbidden, and conspired together for sin and wrong doing and disobedience to the messenger (Muhammad). **And when they come to you, they greet you with a greeting wherewith Allah greets you not**, and say within themselves: 'Why should Allah punish us not for what we say?' Hell will be sufficient for them, they will burn therein, and worst indeed is that destination*".(Allah is mindful of how Muhammad is greeted or saluted. Thus he rebukes the hypocrites for an improper salutation toward Muhammad, and threatens them with the possible punishment of hell fire.)

- Surah 60:12, "*O Prophet! When believing women come to you to give you the pledge of fealty, that they will not associate anything in worship with Allah, ... and that they will not disobey you in any good deed, then accept their fealty, and ask Allah to forgive them...*" (In this verse, Allah is telling Muhammad that when he intercedes, forgiveness will be granted.)

- Surah 33:56, "*Allah sends his prayers on the prophet, and also his angels too. O you who believe, pray for the prophet and greet him with the Islamic way of greeting.*" (Not only Allah would pray for Muhammad but requires that of the angels and the entire Muslim community.)

5. Allah & Muhammad Co-Legislators

The Islamic Shariah is ordained not only by Allah but jointly between Allah and Muhammad. In fact, much of the Shariah is derived from the Sunnah/Hadith as the Qur'an is silent on many issues.

- Surah 9:29, "*Fight against those who believe not in Allah, nor in the Last Day, nor forbid that which has been **forbidden by Allah and his messenger...***" (Allah and Muhammad are co-legislators in all matters.)

- Surah 9:1, "*Freedom from (all) obligations **is declared from Allah and his messenger** to those of the disbelievers in the oneness of Allah, with whom you made a treaty.*"

- Surah 9:3, "***And a declaration from Allah and his messenger** to mankind on the greatest day (of the Hajj) that Allah is free from all obligations to the unbelievers and so is his messenger...*" (Both here and in 9:1 Allah and his messenger are co-legislators and all declarations are issued jointly.)

- Surah 2:279, "*And if you do not do it, then **take a notice of war from Allah and his messenger**...*" (This refers to a joint declaration of war from Allah and Muhammad. All Qur'anic declarations are a form of legislation.)

- Surah 33:36, "*It is not for a believer, man or woman, **when Allah and his messenger have decreed a matter** that they have no option in their decision. And **whoever disobeys Allah and his messenger**, he has indeed strayed in a plain error.*" (Again, Allah and Muhammad are co-legislators, so that Muslims have no choice in matters decreed jointly by Allah and Muhammad.)

6. Allah's Terror Visited on Those who Disobey Muhammad

Obedience to Allah through Muhammad has its rewards as given above. But disobedience against Muhammad has its severe punishments. In fact, the various anti-blasphemy laws in some Muslim countries are derived from the established principle that any belittling or vexing of Muhammad in any form or shape risks capital punishment. In what follows here we are not providing any comments with the Ayah's that are presented. They are clear.

- Surah 58:5, "*Indeed those who oppose Allah and his messenger will be abased, just as those before them were abased. And we have revealed clear signs, and for those who disbelieve there is a humiliating penalty.*"

- Surah 58.20, "*Those who oppose Allah and his messenger, they will be among the most humiliated (i.e. their lives would be made intolerably impossible).*"

- Surah 58.22, "*You (Muhammad) will not find a people who believe in Allah and the last day loving those who oppose Allah and his messenger, even though they were their fathers or their sons or their brothers or their clan...*"

- Surah 59:4, "*That is because they opposed Allah and his messenger. And whosoever opposes Allah, then Allah is severe in punishment.*"

- Surah 4:14, "*And whosoever disobeys Allah and his messenger, and transgresses his limits, he will cast him into the fire, to abide therein; and he shall have a disgraceful torment.*"

- Surah 48:29, "*Muhammad is the messenger of Allah, and those who are with him are ruthless against disbelievers, and merciful among themselves...*"

- Surah 8:12 – 13, "*12 (Remember) when your Lord inspired the angels, 'I am with you, so keep firm those who have believed. I will cast terror into the hearts of those who have disbelieved, so strike them over the necks, and smite over all their fingers and toes.' 13 This is because they defied and disobeyed Allah and his messenger. And whoever defies and disobeys Allah and his messenger, then Allah is severe in punishment.*"

- Surah 9:62 -63, "*62 They swear by Allah to you (Muslims) in order to please you, but it is more fitting that they should please Allah and his messenger, if they are believers. 63 Know they not that whoever opposes and shows hostility to Allah and his messenger, certainly for him will be the fire of hell to abide therein. That is extreme disgrace.*"

- Surah 33:57, "*Those who annoy Allah and his messenger Allah has cursed them in this world, and in the hereafter, and has prepared for them a humiliating torment.*"

- Surah 5:33, "*The recompense **of those who wage war against Allah and his messenger** and do mischief in the land is only that they shall be killed or crucified or their hands and their feet be cut off on the opposite sides, or be exiled from the land...*"

7. Total Inseparability between Allah and Muhammad

The eminent Muslim scholar Ibn Taymiyyah's conclusion which he substantiates with ample Qur'anic references is that,

> "...Allah has substituted Muhammad for Himself in all matters for commanding and forbidding, and revealing. No distinction is allowed to be made between Allah and his Messenger in any of these matters."

This demonstrates the inseparability between Allah and Muhammad on all matters, and establishes this inseparability as a core Islamic doctrine.

In what follows, we list some Qur'anic references, which further support and substantiate the above mentioned notion. For example, in Surah 9:94, the Qur'an asserts that Allah and Muhammad will observe and judge the deeds of people. Islamically speaking, Qur'anic revelations are eternal. Hence, this assertion is timeless and not limited to the time when Muhammad was alive.

- Surah 9:94, "*They will make excuses to you when you have returned to them. Say, 'Make no excuse - never will we believe you. Allah has already informed us of your news. **And Allah will observe your deeds, and so will his messenger**; then you will be taken back to the knower of the unseen and the witnessed, and he will inform you of what you used to do.'*"

- Surah 9:1, "*Freedom from (all) obligations (is declared) from **Allah and his messenger** to those of the disbelievers in the Oneness of Allah, with whom you made a treaty.*"

- Surah 9:3, "*And a declaration from **Allah and his messenger** to mankind on the greatest day (the Hajj) that Allah is free from all obligations to the unbelievers and so is his messenger... And give tidings (O Muhammad) of a painful torment to those who disbelieve.*"

- Surah 9:59, "*Would that they were contented with what **Allah and his messenger** gave them and had said: 'Allah is Sufficient for us. **Allah will give us of his bounty, and also his messenger...**'*"

- Surah 9:61, "*And among them are men who hurt the Prophet and say: 'He is lending his ear to every news; Say: 'He listens to what is best for you; he believes in Allah; has faith in the believers; and is a mercy to those of you who believe.' But those who hurt Allah's messenger will have a painful torment.*"

- Surah 24:51, "*The only saying of the faithful believers, when they are called to **Allah and his messenger**, to judge between them, is that they say: 'We hear and we obey.' And such are the prosperous ones.*"

- Surah 33:57, "*Those who annoy **Allah and his messenger**, Allah has cursed them in this world, and in the Hereafter, and has prepared for them a humiliating torment.*"

- Surah 5:33, "*The recompense of those who wage war against **Allah and his messenger** and spread corruption in the land is only that they shall be killed or crucified or their hands and their feet be cut off on the opposite sides, or be exiled from the land. That is their disgrace in this world, and a great torment is theirs in the Hereafter.*"

- Surah 59:7, "*What Allah gave as booty to his messenger from the people of the townships, - it is for Allah, his messenger, the kindred (of Muhammad), the orphans, the poor, and the wayfarer, in order that it may not become a fortune used by the rich among you. And **whatsoever the messenger gives you, take it, and whatsoever he forbids you, abstain from it**, and fear Allah. Allah is severe in punishment.*" (Rules for distributing war booty are jointly established by Allah and Muhammad.)

The following two Surah's illustrate how Muhammad is given an elevated role reserved only to one with a divine nature, thus giving him an indirect position of inseparability from Allah as affirmed by Muslim scholars.

- Surah 62:2, "*It is He who has raised up from among the common people a **messenger** from among them, to recite his signs to them and **to purify them**, and to teach them the book and the wisdom, though before that they were in manifest error.*"

- Surah 9:128, "*Now has come to you a messenger from amongst yourselves: it grieves him that you should perish: ardently anxious is he over you: to the believers is he most kind and merciful.*"

Chapter 6
Historical Flashback

The Initial Call (Da'wa)

So, how did this all happen in real-time? And what are the implications for today?

Unfortunately, the only source that the Muslim scholars rely on to provide a presumed historical account of Muhammad's career is given in various versions of what is termed as the "Sirah" (purported biography). This was written well after his death at different times by different authors who relied heavily on oral traditions.[85]

The Sirah is both authoritative, and considered to be somewhat speculative.

In examining these belated chronicles of Muhammad's career, it all started with his initial proclamations of absolute oneness of Allah as in

> Surah 112, "Say: 'He is Allah, One. Allah, the self-sufficient, besought of all. He neither begot, nor was begotten. Nor is there anyone equal to him'",

thus declaring all others as forms of idolatry, and in particular, the divine Sonship of Christ, to be the highest form of idolatry and therefore an unforgivable sin, (called Shirk in Islam).

Immediately, Muhammad would declare and institute the Islamic creed (i.e. statement of faith), the Shahadah, requiring that to be a Muslim, one must by necessity and without compromise, believe in both Allah and Muhammad. And whosoever does not believe in Muhammad, and his divine call as the final prophet is rendered a "Kafir" (meaning apostate) even though he might fully believe in the oneness of Allah.

---

85 Though the earliest Sunni Islam "Sirah" was written some 150 years after the death of Muhammad, it is held by Muslims worldwide as authentic and authoritative. The foundational "Sirah" was written by Ibn Is-haq (https://en.wikipedia.org/wiki/Ibn_Ishaq). But, Ibn Hisham later edited it. However, according to researchers the two are almost the same (https://en.wikipedia.org/wiki/Ibn_Hisham). Later Sirah authors added further details. However, the Shiite sect relies instead on Nahj Al-Balagh written in the 10th century AD (https://en.wikipedia.org/wiki/Nahj_al-Balagha) that covers among others, issues of history, social philosophy, ethics, rhetoric, poetry, literature, prophetology, and imamate, etc.

The Qur'an, redefines the "oneness" of the LORD God of the Bible through the Islamic creed, (the Shahadah) and supporting Surah's so that the worship of Jesus Christ would appear to be the worship of an elevated man (i.e. a partner or associate), and thus "idolatry". This left a question as to how this purged absolute "oneness of Allah" should be worshipped (explained earlier in Chapter 5).

Initially, the pagan Arabs of Mecca were seriously shaken by Muhammad's call (Da'wa), which he started to carry out publicly within the Meccean community after three years (from 610 to 612 AD) of a "private Da'wa" to only his closest associates. Starting the public Da'wa in 612, Muhammad openly attacked the entire concept of idol worship which was the basis of Meccean society.

> Surah 53:19-25, "*19. Have you then considered Al-Lat, and Al-'Uzza (two idols of the pagan Arabs) 20. And Manat (another idol of the pagan Arabs), the other third? 21. Is it for you the males and for Him the females? 22. That indeed is a division most unfair 23. They are but names which you have named, you and your fathers, for which Allah has sent down no authority. They follow but a guess and that which they themselves desire, ...*"

Throughout the year visitors would come to Mecca for worship, purchase of statues of the idol gods, trade and much more, so that the entire Meccean economy had depended on the idol worship. By removing the idols, the cultic intermediaries would become irrelevant, and thus would render the need to make the annual pilgrimage (Hajj) to Mecca unnecessary. As a religious center of Arabia, Mecca was also a cultural center with the annual cultural fair, Ukaz, which took place around the Hajj season. By challenging idol worship, Muhammad was cutting off the past devotions to idols and rallying the people around himself, as a new prophet.

As recorded in the Sirah as well as the Qur'an itself, the Quraish (chief tribe of Mecca) leadership did not accept his prophethood claim. There were many Jews and Christians in Mecca so the pagans were aware of their beliefs especially in regard to the Biblical prophets. Muhammad was put to the challenge: "If you are a true prophet, where are your signs and miracles?", they would ask. Surah 17:90-93 provides one illustration:

> Surah 17:90-93, "*90. And they say: 'We shall not believe in you (O Muhammad), until you cause a spring to gush forth from the earth for us; 91. 'Or you*

have a garden of date-palms and grapes, and cause rivers to gush forth in their midst abundantly; ***92.*** *'Or you cause the heaven to fall upon us in pieces, as you have pretended, or you bring Allah and the angels before (us) face to face;* ***93.*** *'Or you have a house of adornable materials, or you ascend up into the sky, and even then we will put no faith in your ascension until you bring down for us a book that we would read..."*

Muhammad's initial response was that the Qur'an itself was his "miracle" according to the following:

- Surah 17:88, "*Say: 'If the mankind and the Jinns were together to produce the like of this Qur'an, they could not produce the like thereof, even if they helped one another.'*"

- Surah 2:23, "*And if you are in doubt concerning that which we have sent down (i.e. the Qur'an) to our slave (Muhammad), then produce a Surah of the like thereof and call your witnesses besides Allah, if you are truthful.*"

People of the Book: A Necessary Evil?

But to fully consolidate his "prophethood" he needed the consent and approval of the Jews and Christians of his day in order for him to have some form of relevance or standing, or at least not to be completely against them.

In the initial phases, he would describe Jews and Christians apparently positively as the "People of the Book", the custodians of the earlier scriptures: the Tawrat, Zaboor and Injeel. He would go further and praise their prophets elevating them to the level of infallibility[86]. And he would adopt some of their rituals and practices, though altering them to fit his new definition of Allah.

By showing what appeared to be some "agreement" with the beliefs of Jews and Christians, he kept them in the dark, pacified, and thus manipulated them. During those initial stages, they thought he was either on their side to some extent, or at least rather harmless. Then he would carry out the bold stroke to

---

[86] In Biblical Christianity, prophets were not infallible. Because of Adam's sin and resulting fall, and although they were chosen by the LORD God, they were still "sinners" and in all but one case the record shows that they had sinned in various ways. The one exception was Jesus Christ, being the Son of God, who was without sin, and in fact carried the burden of man's sin on the cross as reported in the New Testament.

announce that he, Muhammad, was the direct descendent of Abraham (now renamed Ibrahim) through his son Ishmael (renamed Ismaeel).

In this way, he even managed to mislead King Negos of Ethiopia by instructing his followers to quote an ambiguous and a selected half-quotation from a Qur'anic text which gave a strong impression of affirming the core Christian belief in Christ as a "Word of God" though in a different but concealed or veiled sense. Hence it was (allegedly) reported that King Negos, in hearing this apparent "affirmation", drew a line in the sand and stated, "the difference between you (Muslims) and us (Christians) is only as wide as this line." This resulted in the immediate granting of asylum for the early Muslim community refugees in Ethiopia, as they were being strenuously opposed by the Meccans at that time. This maneuvering was initially handled skillfully with the Ethiopian Christians through showing good intentions while hiding the ulterior ones through partial quotations from the Qur'an.

Several years later Muhammad would emigrate with his followers to Yathrib, change its name to Medina (city of the prophet), and immediately establish his political leadership of that city—which was composed of two major pagan Arab tribes (and several other minor pagan Arab tribes) that were all Islamized, and three prominent Arab Jewish tribes[87]. For the first two years in Medina he operated under the so-called "Medina Pact" which gave the impression of a pluralistic society under his leadership.

But, at the point that he had become strong militarily, he would confront the first of three Jewish tribes with his claim to have been included in their scriptures as the "expected one". When the first tribe replied that they found no such reference, they were threatened and exiled. Subsequently, the second tribe was harshly treated and exiled, but the third tribe was dealt with even more brutally by execution and enslavement.[88] [Ref. 6]

A year later he dealt with the Jews of Khyber differently, and in a way that would change history. In the aftermath of the defeat or exile of the first three Medina tribes, Muhammad had found it difficult to run the society because of lack of experience by the nascent Muslim community.

---

87 Historically, the Jews were the founders of Yathrib [Ref. 6]
88 This happened to Banu Quraiza, the third Jewish tribe, whereby all the men, ages 12 and above were executed and the women and children taken as slaves.

So in Khyber, Muhammad relented on the three earlier choices given to the Medina tribes to either accept him as their prophet, face the sword, or be exiled—and instead implemented a fourth option, one that would provide societal containment for those Jews and Christians who refused, thus retaining their skills and fortunes to the service of Islam, but under severe constraints.[89]

That fourth option would be to submit to the political and legal authority of Islam, whereby they could "keep their religion" within severe regulations. Those regulations had and have a legal term, called, "Dhimmitude"[90], whereby Jews and Christians were declared to be legally and morally unequal to Muslims, were forced to agree not to proselytize (under penalty of death), and to pay the Jizyah tax in a state of humiliation, among other severe regulations (Surah 9:29).

After dealing with the Jewish presence in Arabia, and after conquering Mecca in a triumphal return as their prophet/ruler—he would deal rather differently with the Christians of Arabia, but the end would be the same. In a famous encounter with the Christian leadership of Najran, and after a 3 day theological debate, he would impose the Dhimmitude status upon them as well, setting the precedent for how to deal with conquered peoples as Islam would begin to move out of Arabia into the nearby countries.[91] However, before he died he would abolish the Dhimmitude option in Arabia requiring "no two religions in Arabia."

No Two Religions in Arabia and the Islamic "Futuhat" Expansions

The imposition of the directive that only Muslims should reside in the lands of the Arabian Peninsula has been established on the basis of the Sunnah as illustrated in Hadith's 45.17 and 45.18[92] and fully implemented later by the 2nd Khalifah, Omar:

---

89 Pagans had only two choices: accepting Islam (reverting back to Islam, as everyone is born a Muslim as per the Fitrah) or the sword.

90 A key reference on this topic with substantial documentation is: Bat Ye'or: **The Dhimmi: Jews and Christians Under Islam**(http://www.amazon.com/Dhimmi-Jews-Christians-Under-Islam/dp/0838632629/ref=sr_1_6?ie=UTF8&qid=1449522790&sr=8-6&keywords=Bat+Ye'or)

91 See Al-Maqdisi and Solomon, "Al-Yahud: Eternal Islamic Enmity and the Jews." ANM Publishers, 2010.

92 For details see http://islamqa.info/en/47736 which is an official Fatwa in response to the question, "Is it permissible for a non-Muslim to enter Madeenah?"

- Hadith 45.17 (Al-Muwatta Hadith), " ... *One of the last things that the Messenger of Allah, ... said was, 'May Allah fight the Jews and the Christians. They took the graves of their Prophets as places of prostration. Two deens (religions) shall not co-exist in the land of the Arabs.'"*

- Hadith 45.18 (another Al-Muwatta Hadith), *"...Two deens (religions) shall not co-exist in the Arabian Peninsula."*

So what was this all about?

Initially but eventually, Muhammad's message and mission was first remedial, then final and universal:

> Surah 7:158, *"Say (O Muhammad): 'O mankind: I am sent to you all as the Messenger of Allah'..."*

This Surah was used initially to rally the community of the Arabs to Islam, and subsequently to impose it over all mankind starting with the people and nations of the 7th century through letters of "invitation" to Islam, followed by conquest (called the "Al-Futuhat", literally "the openings") and beyond until the present day.

This "Al-Futuhat" concept is expressed in a revealed, thus "divine" Qur'anic term (Surah 48:1, *"We (Allah) have opened for you a manifest opening (victory)[93]."* This doctrine of essentially "sanitized conquest", was imposed by Allah on the Muslim community granting his authority and mandating the need to forcefully convert[94], Islamize and subjugate non-Muslims and their territories.

These conquests, though portrayed by Muslim apologists as "defensive" or otherwise in some form of a positive light, were brutally violent. Muslims and their proponents would declare that by invading territories and subjugating the people under Islam, everyone would have the opportunity to "return" to their Fitrah nature, i.e. Islam. In reality it was a strategic Islamization process that would slowly but surely transform these societies and accomplish the spread of Islam. Thus the "Futuhat", was used to justify and explain the initial con-

---

93 In explaining the concept of the "Futuhat" (the openings) it is important to note the Arabic text as it uses terms derived from the root verb "fataha, to open" or the associated noun "fat-h, opening".
94 Muslims would use the term "revert" rather than "convert" since every human, by nature, is a Muslim, as per the Fitrah doctrine (Surah 30:30)

quest and subjugation of the peoples in the Middle East, North Africa, Spain, Persia, India and parts of China from 634 AD till 710 AD and beyond.

Then, and up until today, the implementation of the "Al-Futuhat" remains in effect, and has inevitably resulted in the Islamization of subsequent territories under the doctrines of Jihad, to bring all people "back" to the "Tawheed", the original doctrine of Islamic Monotheism.

Chapter 7

The Demise of "Similarity"

The Demise of "Similarity": Putting "Sameness" to Rest

We have established from the primary sources of Islam that through the appropriation and recasting of our Biblical narrative in all of its elements, vocabulary and terminology, into the Qur'an itself—that there has been an usurpation of the authentic Biblical narrative which is historically accurate, and proven by fulfillment of its prophecies as well as substantiated by archeology and related disciplines.

The Islamic counter narrative (with its various threads) has been cleverly woven together, by keeping some apparent similarities in the names and stories of the Biblical characters, thus giving the illusion that they are the same as the Biblical ones. Having done that, the Qur'an takes the bold step of declaring that "your God and our Allah are the same." Built into that in the Qur'anic narrative is the unsubstantiated assertion that all previous "books" were earlier limited editions of the Qur'an, that their recipients were all Muslims and that they already knew about Muhammad and paid allegiance to him by Allah's command. The result is a narrative that replaces the Biblical narrative that points to Christ, to another pointing to Muhammad.

This has produced a system that claims to be the same as the one that Christians hold—but which transforms the understanding of both God and His relationship with mankind, in other words, the LORD God's knowability through self revelation and the incarnation. It substitutes Sonship with slavery. Believers are not redeemed through the cross of Christ, but are held captive and in servitude, thus reversing the understanding of the LORD God as a loving Father, into a harsh and cruel master.

As a result, we have demonstrated that the attractions of "similarity" and "sameness" which appear in the Qur'an are nothing but a mirage intended to validate the counterclaims of Islam and its prophet. Unfortunately, this very effective mirage has attracted well-meaning Christian theologians and scholars in their determination to find a common ground through what some have termed "sufficient similarity", from which they endeavor to engage Muslims and bring them to Christ. We hope that this grave and counterproductive missiological misunderstanding will finally be put to rest once and for all.

"Sameness" and Biblical Corruption Tied to the Islamic Narrative

We show that one cannot argue that the Qur'an does not claim Biblical corruption—although a large number of Christian scholars have declared that to be the case. Since the Qur'an speaks of the Tawrat, Zaboor and Injeel, and that Jews and Christians in Muhammad's time were urged to examine their own scriptures—this then was taken as proof for some Christians that the Qur'an acknowledges the "earlier revelations" as being divine and without corruption.

We have shown that these very Qur'anic verses that these Christians have used to illustrate their point, are in reality a stern rebuke, if not a threat, to Jews and Christians of Muhammad's time and hence for eternity. These Jews and Christians were urged to examine "their own books" specifically to discover all the prophecies about Muhammad—not only his expected coming, but the details of his personality and message, together with the Islamic messages that all their prophets had allegedly preached.

Not only did the Tawrat, Zaboor and Injeel confirm the coming of Muhammad, they "came down" from the "Eternal Tablet" thus declaring that they were earlier and limited versions of the Qur'an! By taking that position, the new Islamic narrative was made to hold together by showing how and why our Bible has been corrupted. It involved a completely new revelation process whereby Allah was said to have delivered his "will", composed of demands and directives, through the process of the "Wahy."

Thus it was not just the issue of Biblical corruption per se, but the recasting of the entire narrative to show that the message of "Islamic Monotheism" was the only true message. This necessitated the eventual coming of Muhammad, linking this monotheism with the Islamic creed, the Shahadah, *"No god but Allah and Muhammad is the messenger of Allah."* In so doing the Biblical characters became Qur'anic ones! They were given Arabized/Islamized names, changed stories with changed outcomes. This is usually set aside in favor of the mindset of "sufficient similarity" used by so many Christian scholars. We saw in the Qur'an the omissions, denials and changes made to the stories of Adam, Noah, Abraham, Moses, and Jesus—a recasting to prove that they were, after all, true Muslims who in the final analysis acknowledged Muhammad and bowed to his authority.

The Reality about Allah

Given this reconstructed narrative, the dilemma that faced Islam was, and continues to be, to try to keep an apparent link with the LORD God of the Judeo-Christian scriptures based on the "sameness" declaration, while at the same time calling for "peace" between Muslims and Christians. This so-called "theology" gets wrapped in a political goal with a hidden agenda. Thus in the "Common Word" movement, 138 Muslim scholars representing almost all the main Islamic schools and movements, would venture to make a "peace" offer—one that would look sincere on face value but is very cynical in reality. They would accomplish this by using the Qur'anic verse,

> 3:64, "*Say (O' Muhammad), 'O People of the Scripture, come to a common word between us and you - that we will not worship except Allah and not associate any partner with him and not take one another as lords besides Allah.' But if they turn away, then say that you bear witness that we are Muslims.*"

The Common Word invitation would focus on the "unity of God," declaring in another form the sameness between Allah of Islam and the LORD God of the Bible. What is hidden in the peace offer is that in reality it is a veiled threat—a modern form of the very threat from Muhammad to Emperor Heraclius of Byzantium in 628 AD. Using the same Qur'anic verse, i.e. 3:64, Emperor Heraclius was "invited to the message of Islam" and told in no uncertain terms, "be a Muslim and you will be safe (Aslim Tislam)."

Based on all these factors and more, it became incumbent on us to try to describe who Allah is and is not. We showed that because of the various Qur'anic injunctions on the nature of Allah (or rather the lack of any comprehensible nature using human understanding), Muslim scholars have had immense difficulties in coming to grips with this thorny question. At one point "Allah is All and All is Allah." At another point this statement is negated.

In order the keep some level of unity among the scholars, the final words of wisdom on this issue came about by defining four basic negatives about him—all in support of the Qur'anic assertion, "… *there is none like him* …" But these deductions would further emphasize and remove all possibilities about the knowledge of Allah: In the end, Allah is genderless, although called "he;" and his "oneness" cannot be described as one in number, form, substance, essence, etc. Although he is called "the creator", his creation was brought into being remotely, without his personal involvement with his creation. He is a distant creator, in another realm since he would never reveal himself, make man in his image, or make conditional and unconditional covenants with man. He is said to be absolute in power, yet limited. He is unaccountable.

Dire Implications

The conclusion is that Islamic thought and practice has constructed a formidable system of enslavement and constitutional discrimination from which there is little room to move or chance of escape, humanly speaking. This system could not be the product of the loving LORD God who revealed Himself as the Father, who sent "*His only begotten Son that whoever believes in Him shall not perish but have eternal life.*" (John 3:16) Surely this system of bondage, deception, and divinely ordained enmity of the "other", could never reflect the character and nature of the LORD God of the Bible—the Triune God, who is the covenant making, the covenant keeping, the covenant sustaining God, the God who revealed Himself fully in Christ Jesus—who came to set the captives free. (Isaiah 61:1a, Luke 4:18)

To put it in hypothetical terms, if Allah were one and the same as the LORD God of the Bible, then he would have also been the father of our Lord Jesus Christ, such that it would have been impossible for him to deny the salvific mission of His only begotten son, His crucifixion, His burial, His resurrection, His ascension, and His glorious return.

So, Where do We Go from Here?

Therefore, the only conclusive and meaningful yardstick for measurement and examination of the sameness or differences between the LORD God of the Bible and the Allah of the Qur'an must be the person, the message, and the mission of

Christ Jesus—for He is the fulfillment of the law, the prophets, the Psalms, and the totality of the scriptures, as incomparably expressed in Colossians 1:15-19.

The scripture declares that Christ is the image of the invisible God,

> *[15] **The Son is the image of the invisible God**, the firstborn over all creation. [16] For in Him all things were created: things in heaven and on earth, visible and invisible, whether thrones or powers or rulers or authorities; all things have been created through Him and for Him. [17] He is before all things, and in him all things hold together. [18] And he is the head of the body, the church; he is the beginning and the firstborn from among the dead, so that in everything he might have the supremacy. [19] For God was pleased to have all his fullness dwell in him, [20] and through him to reconcile to himself all things, whether things on earth or things in heaven, by making peace through his blood, shed on the cross.*

And Jesus said of Himself,

- *"Very truly I tell you," Jesus answered, "before Abraham was born, I am!" (John 8:58)*

- *"I am the alpha and the omega, the alif and the taf. I am the beginning and the end." (Rev. 1:8)*

- *"I and the Father are one…" (John 10:30)*

- *"He who has seen me has seen the Father…" (John 14:9)*

The Bible verses quoted above prove conclusively that the Allah of the Qur'an has no commonality with the LORD God of the Bible, nor does Islamic monotheism (Tawheed) have anything to do with Old or New Testament Biblical monotheism.

As indicated early on in this book, great damage has been and is being done to Christian missions by relying on apparent commonalities and related missiological methodologies based on these assumed similarities—similarities which we have now shown to provide an intentional illusion woven intermittently into the Qur'anic text. Hopefully, this exposure will go a long way to counter such methodologies, so that a Biblical missiological paradigm will be developed to reflect the reality, rather than the illusion.

Finally, the Qur'an can best be described as a set of "...*arguments raised up against the knowledge of God...*" (2 Cor. 10:5)—meaning, arguments against the "knowability" of God.

It behooves us as Christians to heed the advice of the Apostle Paul to consider this spiritual battle to be "*not against flesh and blood, but against the rulers, against the authorities, against the powers of this dark world and against the spiritual forces of evil in the heavenly realms...*" (Eph. 6:12).

Further, by putting on the "*full armor of God*" to "*stand*" against these forces, we are also reminded "*(He) trains my hands for war ...*" (Psalm 144:1), and that our only offensive weapon is "*the sword of the spirit which is the word of God,*" (Eph. 6:17)—hence the necessity of "*rightly dividing the word of truth*" (2 Tim. 15), to "*set the captives free.*" (Luke 4:18)

Appendix

A. Coinage of the Tawheed Term

The Word "Tawheed"[95]

"Tawheed" is a technical Islamic term which is provably coined, meaning it is manmade term expressing certain concepts. And although Tawheed is considered as the central doctrine of Islam, as a word or a term it does not occur anywhere in the Qur'an.

Tawheed is an Arabic word which is a strictly technical term in the Islamic lexicon. From a linguistic point of view Tawheed is a "verbal noun"[96] which is extracted from the noun, (wahed وَاحِدٌ) and its various verbal tense formats, past (wahhada وحّد), present (yuwahhed يوحّد), future (sa-yuwahhed سيوحّد), and the command-operative form (wahhed وحّد). The verbal noun in Arabic usually refers to the doing of the action referred to by the verb.[97]

The root verb Wahhada has a progressive spectrum of meaning: to consolidate, to bring together, to unify, to uphold unity and ultimately to maintain or sustain oneness. Hence it is a verb which initiates successive actions and applications aimed at bringing into being a state of oneness,

In other words, Wahhada itself means "to unite" but in a dynamic way. Hence it is a specialized verb-form which implies immediacy. In essence, it infers the equivalent of an implied command to start a process of "uniting" and "making into one".

This action or dynamic application can be observed in diverse fields or disciplines of life be they visible and tangible, or invisible and intangible such as the assembling of people into workable units, starting from individuals into families, families into tribes and ultimately mobilizing tribes into one

---

95 We use "Tawheed" in this book to correspond to the Arabic/Islamic term: Al-Tawheed, which is pronounced "At-Tawheed" whereby the "l" of the definite article "al" is not pronounced. This is because the letter "t" that follows the "l" of the definite article is a "solar" letter. Half of the Arabic alphabet is "solar" like "t" or "s" and the other half is "lunar" like "k" or "q".
96 See for the example, http://oxforddictionaries.com/definition/english/verbal%2Bnoun
97 http://allthearabicyouneverlearnedthefirsttimearound.com/p2/p2-ch2/verbal-nouns/

unified nation; or, starting from a single individual sportsman to the building up of a team.

Tawheed, a noun coined to specifically express the derived "oneness" nature of Allah, retains the immediacy of its verbal root "wahhada", and thus would in turn infer the starting of a process to bring into unity: unity of understanding, unity of purpose, unity of worship. Using the analogies above of the sports team or the building of a nation, the societal unit would also apply to the consolidation of separate institutions into a single unified institution by design, such as the consolidation of army divisions into battalions, then into an army, or the police and intelligence services into a law enforcement agency.

Therefore, we see that Wahhada or Tawheed can and does also apply to the unification of systems. A simple example would be when a municipality in a given city would build a centrally unified system for the collection and distribution of water to all residences, businesses and industries, or a system for processing waste water and so on. A more complex example would be an interconnected electric power grid for a region, an entire country or in some cases an entire continent. Such a grid would entail the complex design of a unified system of electricity generating plants of various sources of energy (like hydro, coal, oil, gas, solar, wind, and nuclear), small and large, interconnected through thousands of transformers, millions of meters, and a vast web of thousands of miles of cables and wires—linked together by communication and control systems at every sub-level, and coordinated by a Central Command and Control Center.

An even more global example would be NASA's space program, which is the largest and most extensive interconnected large scale "system" in history.

Wahhada is applicable to concepts and theories as well. In physics a major goal is to come up with a unified theory that would explain all observable phenomena, as derived from the behaviors of subatomic particles to those of planets, stars and galaxies combining such theories as; relativity, quantum mechanics, particle physics, cosmology and so on.

Attempts to Give Meaning to Tawheed

However our subject matter is the unity of Allah, or "Oneness" of the Islamic god. As such our first task is to examine the primary sources of Islam in regard to its teaching on the being of Allah, which in turn was compounded by Muslim scholars through long deliberations, arguments counter arguments and speculations. These led them to formulate *by deduction* the formation of the doctrine of oneness of Allah or Tawheed.

But why and what led to such arguments and counter arguments with long deliberations?

Equally why was it necessary to formulate this concept by deduction? Isn't Tawheed recorded clearly in the Qur'an?

So before we introduce the reader to the primary sources of Islam, it is important to state a brief response to the foregoing issues: as Tawheed is a verbal noun that comes from the verbal root 'wahhada' to unify, to consolidate or to unite, to form into one. It immediately becomes strikingly clear that the Islamic doctrine of Tawheed, strange as it may sound, is manmade and not "divine," i.e. clearly not reported as a term in the Islamic primary sources.

For example the word "Islam" (Surah's 3:19, 3:85) and "Muslim" (Surah 22:78, "It is He Who has named you Muslims …") are divinely coined and sanctioned words; so are the many "names" of Allah as well as those of Muhammad (as given in Chapter 4). In other words the stated or revealed concepts of Allah, the Islamic god, in the primary sources of Islam are far from unified and in fact are quite diverse, thus requiring scholars to synthesize alternative understandings of it.

To sum up, we see that "Tawheed" as a technical Islamic term is provably a coined term, meaning it is manmade expressing certain concepts. And although Tawheed is considered as the central doctrine of Islam, as a word or a term it does not occur anywhere either in the Qur'an or the Sunnah.

However what does occur are four variations of the word "One" (وٱحد) and one variation of the term "One alone," (وٱحده). Here are the actual related terms/words on this issue given in the Qur'an:

1. The word "wahed" (وٱحد) meaning one is used for both Allah and for other generic purposes—such as "one kind of food, (Surah 2:61)", "one door, (Surah 12:67)", "each one 24:2", etc. However when

referring to Allah this form appears in some 13 Qur'anic verses (see the table below).

2. The word "al-wahed" (أَلْوَاحِد) meaning "the one" with a definite article for Allah appears some 6 times, whereby in all such cases Allah is described as "the vanquisher".

3. Then the word "wahedan" (وَاحِدأ) being a variation of "one" as the "object" in the sentence which appears 3 times only.

4. The word "ahad" (أَحَدٌ) used once positively (Surah 112:1) and once negatively in the same (Surah112:4).

5. The "No deity except 'he'" (لا إِلـه إِلَّا هُو) occurs 6 times as an adjective for Allah in verses of threat or intimidation (to others to accept Islam)

The table below provides the specific Aya's (Qur'anic verses) for all such 29 occurrences related to Allah being "one," with some indication of the nature of Allah's oneness.

Earlier we asked the question, "why was it necessary to invent or coin a new term (Tawheed)?" Herein we have shown part of the reason in that there occurs no expression for Tawheed in the Qur'an thus necessitating a clarification. To express and maintain the absolute monotheism as well as keeping or realizing the totality of separation of Allah from his creation obligated and forced the coinage of the term "Tawheed."

We say "absolute monotheism," to explain "Tawheed." An noted in Chapter 4 this is because there is a huge variation or rather a spectrum of variations amongst some of the most notable Muslim scholars, both ancient and modern, in their views and explanations of the doctrine of Tawheed.

Term Referring to "one" Allah	Occurrence in the Qur'an	No. of Occurrences
One/Ahad أَحَدٌ	1. 112:1: قُلْ هُوَ اللَّهُ أَحَدٌ (Say: he is Allah, the one and only) 2. 112:4: وَلَمْ يَكُنْ لَهُ كُفُوًا أَحَدٌ (And there is none like unto him)	1 Positive 1 Negative
One/Wahed وَاحِدٌ	1. 2:163: ... وَإِلَٰهُكُمْ إِلَٰهٌ وَاحِدٌ لَا إِلَٰهَ إِلَّا هُوَ الرَّحْمَٰنُ الرَّحِيمُ...(... And your god is one god ...) 2. 4:171: ... إِنَّمَا اللَّهُ إِلَٰهٌ وَاحِدٌ ... (...for Allah is one god ...) 3. 5:73: ... وَمَا مِنْ إِلَٰهٍ إِلَّا إِلَٰهٌ وَاحِدٌ...(... for there is no god except one ...) 4. 6:19: ... قُلْ إِنَّمَا هُوَ إِلَٰهٌ وَاحِدٌ ... (...for he is one god ...) 5. 14:52: ... وَلِيَعْلَمُوا أَنَّمَا هُوَ إِلَٰهٌ وَاحِدٌ ... (...for he is one god ...) 6. 16:22: ... إِلَٰهُكُمْ إِلَٰهٌ وَاحِدٌ...(...Your god is one god ...) 7. 16:51: ... إِنَّمَا هُوَ إِلَٰهٌ وَاحِدٌ ... (...for Allah is one god ...) 8. 18:110 ... أَنَّمَا إِلَٰهُكُمْ إِلَٰهٌ وَاحِدٌ ... (...for your god is one god ...) 9. 21:108: ... أَنَّمَا إِلَٰهُكُمْ إِلَٰهٌ وَاحِدٌ ... (...for your god is one god ...) 10. 22:34: ... فَإِلَٰهُكُمْ إِلَٰهٌ وَاحِدٌ...(...for your god is one god ...) 11. 29:46: ... وَإِلَٰهُنَا وَإِلَٰهُكُمْ وَاحِدٌ...(...and our god and yours is one ...) 12. 37:4: إِنَّ إِلَٰهَكُمْ لَوَاحِدٌ(Your god is but one) 13. 41:6: ... أَنَّمَا إِلَٰهُكُمْ إِلَٰهٌ وَاحِدٌ ... (...for your god is one god ...)	13

The One/ Al-Wahed أَلْوَاحِدُ	1. 12:39: ... أَمِ ٱللَّهُ ٱلْوَاحِدُ ٱلْقَهَّارُ (...or one Allah, supreme and vanquisher?) 2. 13:16: ... وَهُوَ ٱلْوَاحِدُ ٱلْقَهَّارُ (He is this one, the supreme and vanquisher.) 3. 14:48: ... وَبَرَزُواْ لِلَّهِ ٱلْوَاحِدِ ٱلْقَهَّارِ (... they appeared before Allah, the one, the vanquisher) 4. 38:65: ... وَمَا مِنْ إِلَهٍ إِلَّا ٱللَّهُ ٱلْوَاحِدُ ٱلْقَهَّارُ ... and there is no god except Allah, the one, the vanquisher) 5. 38:4: ... سُبْحَانَهُ هُوَ ٱللَّهُ ٱلْوَاحِدُ ٱلْقَهَّارُ (... he is Allah, the one, the vanquisher) 6. 40:16: ... ٱلْمُلْكُ ٱلْيَوْمَ لِلَّهِ ٱلْوَاحِدِ ٱلْقَهَّارِ (... the dominion today is for Allah, the one, the vanquisher)	6
One/Wahidan وَاحِدًا	1. 2: 133: قَالُواْ نَعْبُدُ إِلَهَكَ وَإِلَهَ آبَائِكَ إِبْرَاهِيمَ وَإِسْمَاعِيلَ وَإِسْحَاقَ إِلَهًا وَاحِدًا(...They said we worship your god and the god of your fathers, Ibrahim, Ismaeel, and Is-haaq—as one god, and we submit to him as Muslims) 2. 9:31: ... وَمَا أُمِرُواْ إِلَّا لِيَعْبُدُواْ إِلَهًا وَاحِدًا ...(... and have they not been commanded but to worship one god ...) 3. 38:5: ... أَجَعَلَ ٱلْآلِهَةَ إِلَهًا وَاحِدًا (Has he made all the gods into one god?)	3
One alone/Wahdahu وحده	1. 7:70: ... قَالُوٓاْ أَجِئْتَنَا لِنَعْبُدَ ٱللَّهَ وَحْدَهُ (They (pagan Arabs) said, did we come to worship Allah alone...) 2. 39:45: ... وَإِذَا ذُكِرَ ٱللَّهُ وَحْدَهُ (And if Allah alone is mentioned ...)	5

	3. 40:12 ...ذَٰلِكُم بِأَنَّهُ إِذَا دُعِيَ ٱللَّهُ وَحْدَهُ (when Allah alone was invoked as the object of worship ...)
	4. 40:84 ...قَالُوا ءَامَنَّا بِٱللَّهِ وَحْدَهُ (But when they saw Our determined might, they said: "We believe in Allah alone ...)
	5. 60:4 ...وَبَدَا بَيْنَنَا وَبَيْنَكُمُ ٱلْعَدَاوَةُ وَٱلْبَغْضَاءُ أَبَداً حَتَّىٰ تُؤْمِنُوا بِٱللَّهِ وَحْدَهُ... (and there has arisen, between us and you, enmity and hatred for ever,- unless ye believe in Allah and Him alone ...)

Negation of more than one god	Occurrence in the Qur'an
No god but he لَا إِلَٰهَ إِلَّا هُوَ	1. 2:255, ٱللَّهُ لَا إِلَٰهَ إِلَّا هُوَ ٱلْحَيُّ ٱلْقَيُّومُ.... (Allah! There is no god but he, the living, the self-subsisting, Eternal ...)
	2. 3:2, ٱللَّهُ لَا إِلَٰهَ إِلَّا هُوَ ٱلْحَيُّ ٱلْقَيُّومُ (Allah! There is no god but He,-the living, the self-subsisting, Eternal.)
	3. 3:6, هُوَ ٱلْعَزِيزُ ٱلْحَكِيمُهُوَ ٱلَّذِي يُصَوِّرُكُمْ فِي ٱلْأَرْحَامِ كَيْفَ يَشَاءُ لَاإِلَٰهَ إِلَّا (He it is who shapes you in the wombs as he pleases. There is no god but he, the exalted in might, the wise.)
	4. 3:18, شَهِدَ ٱللَّهُ أَنَّهُ لَا إِلَٰهَ إِلَّا هُوَ وَٱلْمَلَائِكَةُ وَأُولُوا ٱلْعِلْمِ قَائِماً بِٱلْقِسْطِ لَا إِلَٰهَ إِلَّا هُوَ ٱلْعَزِيزُ ٱلْحَكِيمُ (There is no god but he: That is the witness of Allah, His angels, and those endued with knowledge, standing firm on justice. There is no god but He, the Exalted in Power, the Wise.)
	5. 3:62. إِنَّ هَٰذَا لَهُوَ ٱلْقَصَصُ ٱلْحَقُّ وَمَا مِنْ إِلَٰهٍ إِلَّا ٱللَّهُ وَإِنَّ ٱللَّهَ لَهُوَ ٱلْعَزِيزُ ٱلْحَكِيمُ (This is the true account: There is no god except Allah; andee is indeed the exalted in power, the wise.)
	6. 4:87, ٱللَّهُ لَا إِلَٰهَ إِلَّا هُوَ لَيَجْمَعَنَّكُمْ إِلَىٰ يَوْمِ ٱلْقِيَامَةِ لَا رَيْبَ فِيهِ وَمَنْ أَصْدَقُ مِنَ ٱللَّهِ حَدِيثاً (Allah! There is no god but he: of a surety he

Negation of more than one god	Occurrence in the Qur'an
	will gather you together against the day of judgment, about which there is no doubt. And whose word can be truer than Allah's?)
	7. 7:158, قُلْ يَا أَيُّهَا النَّاسُ إِنِّي رَسُولُ اللهِ إِلَيْكُمْ جَمِيعاً الَّذِي لَهُ مُلْكُ السَّمَاوَاتِ وَالأَرْضِ لا إِلَـهَ إِلاَّ هُوَ يُحْيِـي وَيُمِيتُ فَآمِنُواْ بِاللهِ وَرَسُولِهِ النَّبِيِّ الأُمِّيِّ الَّذِي يُؤْمِنُ بِاللهِ وَكَلِمَاتِهِ وَاتَّبِعُوهُ لَعَلَّكُمْ تَهْتَدُونَ (Say: "O men! I am sent unto you all, as the messenger of Allah, to whom belongs the dominion of the heavens and the earth: there is no god but he: it is he That gives both life and death. So believe in Allah and his messenger, the unlettered prophet, who believeth in Allah and His words: follow him that (so) ye may be guided.")
	8. 9:31, اتَّخَذُواْ أَحْبَارَهُمْ وَرُهْبَانَهُمْ أَرْبَاباً مِّن دُونِ اللهِ وَالْمَسِيحَ ابْنَ مَرْيَمَ وَمَا أُمِرُواْ إِلاَّ لِيَعْبُدُواْ إِلَـهاً وَاحِداً لاَّ إِلَـهَ إِلاَّ هُوَ سُبْحَانَهُ عَمَّا يُشْرِكُونَ (They take their priests and their monks to be their lords in derogation of Allah, and (they take as their Lord) Christ the son of Mary; yet they were commanded to worship but one Allah: there is no god but he. Praise and glory to him: (Far is he) from having the partners they associate (with him).)
	9. 9:129, فَإِن تَوَلَّوْاْ فَقُلْ حَسْبِيَ اللهُ لا إِلَـهَ إِلاَّ هُوَ عَلَيْهِ تَوَكَّلْتُ وَهُوَ رَبُّ الْعَرْشِ الْعَظِيمِ (But if they turn away, Say: "Allah suffices me: there is no god but he: In him is my trust,- he is the Lord of the throne")
	10. 11:14, فَإِن لَّمْ يَسْتَجِيبُواْ لَكُمْ فَاعْلَمُواْ أَنَّمَا أُنزِلَ بِعِلْمِ اللهِ وَأَن لاَّ إِلَـهَ إِلاَّ هُوَ فَهَلْ أَنتُم مُّسْلِمُونَ ("If then they (your false gods) answer not your (call), know that this revelation is sent down with the knowledge of Allah, and that there is no god but he! will you even then submit (to Islam)?")
	11. 13:30, كَذَلِكَ أَرْسَلْنَاكَ فِي أُمَّةٍ قَدْ خَلَتْ مِن قَبْلِهَا أُمَمٌ لِّتَتْلُوَ عَلَيْهِمُ الَّذِي أَوْحَيْنَا إِلَيْكَ وَهُمْ يَكْفُرُونَ بِالرَّحْمَـنِ قُلْ هُوَ رَبِّي لا إِلَـهَ إِلاَّ هُوَ عَلَيْهِ تَوَكَّلْتُ وَإِلَيْهِ مَتَابِ (Thus have we sent thee amongst a People before whom (long since) have (other) Peoples (gone and) passed away; in order that you might rehearse to them what we send down to you by inspiration; yet do they

Negation of more than one god	Occurrence in the Qur'an
	reject (him), the most gracious! Say: "He is my Lord! There is no god but he! In him is my trust, and to him do I turn!")
	12. 16:2 يُنَزِّلُ الْمَلَائِكَةَ بِالرُّوحِ مِنْ أَمْرِهِ عَلَى مَن يَشَاءُ مِنْ عِبَادِهِ أَنْ أَنذِرُواْ أَنَّهُ لَا إِلَهَ إِلَّا أَنَا فَاتَّقُونِ (He sends down his angels with inspiration of his command, to such of his servants as he pleases, (saying): "Warn, that there is no god but I: so do your duty unto me.")

B. Fatwa Regarding the Necessity of Loving Muhammad

Quoted exactly from https://islamqa.info/en/14250

14250: Why do we have to love the Prophet (peace and blessings of Allaah be upon him) more than any other person?

Why do we have to love, obey, follow and venerate our Prophet Muhammad (peace and blessings of Allaah be upon him) the most (or more than any other person)?

Response:

Praise be to Allaah.

1 – Allaah has commanded us to obey the Prophet (peace and blessings of Allaah be upon him). Allaah says (interpretation of the meaning):

"And obey Allaah and the Messenger (Muhammad), and beware (of even coming near to drinking or gambling or Al-Ansaab, or Al-Azlaam) and fear Allaah. Then if you turn away, you should know that it is Our Messenger's duty to convey (the Message) in the clearest way" [al-Maa'idah 5:92]

2 – Allaah has told us that obedience to the Prophet (peace and blessings of Allaah be upon him) is obedience to Allaah. Allaah says (interpretation of the meaning):

"He who obeys the Messenger (Muhammad), has indeed obeyed Allaah, but he who turns away, then we have not sent you (O Muhammad) as a watcher over them" [al-Nisa' 4:80]

3 – Allaah has warned us against failing to obey him, and that this may lead a Muslim into a fitnah that is the fitnah of shirk. Allaah says (interpretation of the meaning):

"Make not the calling of the Messenger (Muhammad) among you as your calling one of another. Allaah knows those of you who slip away under shelter (of some excuse without taking the permission to leave, from the Messenger). And let those who oppose the Messenger's (Muhammad's) commandment (i.e. his Sunnah legal ways, orders, acts of worship, statements) (among the sects) beware, lest some Fitnah (disbelief, trials, afflictions, earthquakes, killing, overpowered by a tyrant) should befall them or a painful torment be inflicted on them" [al-Noor 24:63]

Allaah has told us that the status of Prophethood which he gave to His Prophet (peace and blessings of Allaah be upon him) requires the believers to respect and venerate the Prophet (peace and blessings of Allaah be upon him). Allaah says (interpretation of the meaning):

" , We have sent you (O Muhammad) as a witness, as a bearer of glad tidings, and as a warner.

9. In order that you (O mankind) may believe in Allaah and His Messenger, and that you assist and honour him, and (that you) glorify (Allaah's) praises morning and afternoon" [al-Fath 48:8-9]

4 – The Muslim's faith cannot be complete unless he loves the Prophet (peace and blessings of Allaah be upon him), and until the Prophet (peace and blessings of Allaah be upon him) is dearer to him than his father, his son, his own self and all the people. It was narrated that Anas said: The Prophet (peace and blessings of Allaah be upon him) said: "No one of you truly believes until I am dearer to him than his father, his son, his own self and all the people."

Narrated by al-Bukhaari, 15; Muslim, 44.

It was narrated that 'Abd-Allaah ibn Hishaam said: We were with the Prophet (peace and blessings of Allaah be upon him) when he was holding the hand of 'Umar ibn al-Khattaab. 'Umar said to him: "O Messenger of Allaah, you are dearer to me than everything except my own self." The Prophet (peace and blessings of Allaah be upon him) said: "No, by the One in Whose hand is my soul, not until I am dearer to you than your own self." 'Umar said to him: "Now, by Allaah, you are dearer to me than my own self." The Prophet (peace and blessings of Allaah be upon him) said: "Now (you are a true believer), O 'Umar." Narrated by al-Bukhaari, 6257.

Shaykh al-Islam Ibn Taymiyah (may Allaah have mercy on him) said: The reason why it is obligatory to love the Prophet (peace and blessings of Allaah be upon him) and venerate him more than any other person is that we cannot attain the greatest good in this world or in the Hereafter except at the hands of the Prophet (peace and blessings of Allaah be upon him), by believing in him and following him. That is because no one can be saved from the punishment of Allaah, and the mercy of Allaah cannot reach him except by means of the Prophet, by believing in him, loving him, being loyal to him and following him. This is the means by which Allaah will save him from punishment in this world and in the Hereafter. This is the means by which he will attain what is good in this world and in the Hereafter. The greatest blessing is the blessing of faith, which can only be attained through him, and which is more beneficial than his own self and his wealth. He is the one by means of whom Allaah brings people forth from darkness into light, and there is no other way to Allaah. As for a person's self and family, they will not avail him anything before Allaah… Majmoo' al-Fataawa, 27/246.

One of the scholars said: If a person thinks of the benefits that he has been given through the Prophet (peace and blessings of Allaah be upon him), through whom Allaah brought him forth from the darkness of kufr into the light of faith, he will realize that he is the cause of his soul remaining forever in eternal bliss, and he will understand that this benefit is greater than all others. So he (the Prophet (peace and blessings of Allaah be upon him)) deserves that his share of a person's love should be greater than anyone else's. But people vary with regard to that, depending on the extent to which they bear that in mind or neglect it. Everyone who truly believes in the Prophet (peace and blessings of Allaah be upon him) will inevitably have a strong love for him, but they differ in the extent and depth of their love for him. Some of them have a great deal of love for him and some have only a little, like those who are absorbed in their own whims and desires most of the time. But when mention of the Prophet (peace and blessings of Allaah be upon him) is made, most of them long to see him, and prefers that to their own family, sons, wealth and fathers. But that feeling quickly fades because of other distractions. And Allaah is the One Whose help we seek. See Fath al-Baari, 1/59

This is what is referred to in the verse where Allaah says (interpretation of the meaning):

"The Prophet is closer to the believers than their own selves" [al-Ahzaab 33:6]

Ibn Katheer (may Allaah have mercy on him) said:

[Allaah] knew how compassionate His Messenger (peace and blessings of Allaah be upon him) was towards his Ummah, and how sincere he was towards them, so He made him closer to them than their own selves, and decreed that his judgment among them should take precedence over their own preferences. (6/380).

Shaykh Ibn Sa'di (may Allaah have mercy on him) said:

Allaah tells the believers something by which they may understand the position and status of the Messenger (peace and blessings of Allaah be upon him, so that they might interact with him appropriately. So He said: "The Prophet is closer to the believers than their own selves", the closest that he could be to a person, and closer than his own self. So the Messenger is closer to him than his own self, because he (peace and blessings of Allaah be upon him) was so kind and sincere and compassionate towards them. He was the kindest and most merciful of mankind. The Messenger of Allaah did the greatest of favours to all of mankind. Not the slightest good came to them and not the slightest harm was warded off from them except through him. Hence if there is a conflict between what a person himself wants or what other people want, and what the Messenger wants, then what the Messenger wants must take precedence. What the Messenger says cannot be overridden by what any person says, no matter who he is. They should sacrifice their selves, their wealth and their children, and put love for him before their love for all others.

What the scholars have said may be summed up by noting that the wrath of Allaah and the Fire of Hell are the things that we fear the most, and we cannot be saved from them except at the hands of the Messenger (peace and blessings of Allaah be upon him). The pleasure of Allaah and the garden of Paradise are the things that we want the most, but we cannot attain them except at the hands of the Messenger (peace and blessings of Allaah be upon him).

The Prophet (peace and blessings of Allaah be upon him) referred to the former when he said: "The likeness of me and you is that of a man who lit a fire and grasshoppers and moths started falling into it, and he tried to push them away. I am seizing your waistbands and trying to pull you away from the Fire but you are trying to get away from me."

(Muslim, 2285, from the hadeeth of Jaabir; a similar hadeeth was narrated by al-Bukhaari, 3427 from the hadeeth of Abu Hurayrah).

What is meant by this hadeeth is that the Prophet (peace and blessings of Allaah be upon him) likened the way in which the ignorant and disobedient rush to fall into the Fire of the Hereafter by means of their sins and whims and desires to the

Fire, and their keenness to fall into that Fire, even though he is trying hard to prevent them from doing so to the way in which moths and other insects are fatally attracted to the fire. Both of them are keen to destroy themselves because of their ignorance of the consequences.

(Sharh Muslim by al-Nawawi)

The latter was referred to by the Prophet (peace and blessings of Allaah be upon him) when he said: "All of my Ummah will enter Paradise except those who refuse." They said: "O Messenger of Allaah, who would refuse?" He said: "Whoever obeys me will enter Paradise and whoever disobeys me has refused."

Al-Bukhaari, 7280, from the hadeeth of Abu Hurayrah.

And Allaah is the Source of strength.

Bibliography

1. Sam Solomon, "The Challenge from Islam," Chapter 4 in the book: Ravi Zacharias (Author and General Editor), *Beyond Opinion: Living the Faith We Defend*.

2. Sam Solomon, *A Proposed Charter of Muslim Understanding*, foreword by Gerard Batten, UK Independence Party, Member of the European Parliament for London. 1st Edition—December 2006. Revised Edition—April 2007 www.pilcrowpress.com

3. Sam Solomon and E. Al Maqdisi, *The Mosque and It's Role In Society*, www.pilcrowpress.com, or http://advancingnativemissions.com/store/books/

4. Sam Solomon and E. Al Maqdisi, *The Common Word: The Undermining of the Church*, www.pilcrowpress.com, or http://advancingnativemissions.com/store/books/

5. Sam Solomon and E. Al Maqdisi, *The Modern Day Trojan Horse: Al-Hijra, The Islamic Doctrine of Immigration, Accepting Freedom or Imposing Islam?* www.pilcrowpress.com, or http://advancingnativemissions.com/store/books/

6. E. Al Maqdisi and Sam Solomon, *Al-Yahud: Eternal Islamic Enmity & the Jews*, www.pilcrowpress.com, or http://advancingnativemissions.com/store/books/

7. Paul J. Korshin, *Typologies in England 1650-1820*, Princeton University Press, 1982.

8. John C. Clark & Marcus Peter Johnson, *The Incarnation of God*, Crossway, Wheaton, Illinois, 2015.

9. Richard Booker, *Discovering the Miracle of the Scarlet Thread*, Destiny Image Publishers, 1983.

10. D. A. Carson, *The Scriptures Testify about Me*, Crossway, Wheaton, Illinois, USA, 2013.

11. T. Desmond Alexander, *From Eden to the New Jerusalem: An Introduction to Biblical Theology*, Kregel Publications, UK, 2009.

12. Paul L. Redditt, *Introduction to the Prophets*, Edermans Publishing Co., US and UK, 2008.

13. Mitch and Zhava Glaser, *The Fall Feasts of Israel*, Moody Press, USA, 1987.

14. Ervin N. Hershberger, *Seeing Christ in the Tabernacle*, Vision Publishers, USA, 2007.

15. M. R. DeHaan, *Portraits of Christ in Genesis*, Zondervan Publishing House, USA, 8th printing, 1972.

16. M. R. DeHaan, *The Tabernacle*, Zondervan Publishing House, USA, 8th printing, 1955 and renewed in 1983.

17. David M. Levy, *The Tabernacle: Shadows of the Messiah—Its Sacrifices, Services, and Priesthood*, ISBN-10: 915540-17-7, 1993.

18. William H. Marty, *The Whole Bible Story*, Bethany House Publishers, USA, 2011.

19. Edmund P. Clowney, *The Unfolding Mystery: Discovering Christ in the Old Testament,* ISBN: 978-I-59638-892-5 (pbk), 1988 and 2013.

20. James A. Borland, *Christ in the Old Testament: Old Testament Appearances of Christ in Human Form*, ISBN 978-1-84550-627-8, 2010.

21. Christopher J.H. Wright, *Knowing Jesus through the Old Testament*, Inter Varsity Press, USA (second edition 2014).

22. Qadi Iyad, *Al-Shifa/Huquq Al-Mustafa*, (in Arabic)

23. Shaikh M. B. I. Al-Amrani, et al, *Rights of the Prophet*, (In Arabic) published by Al-Bayan Magazine, 2001.

24. Shaikh M. B. Abdel-Wahhab, *Collected Writings*, (In Arabic). Vol. 1. ISBN 10 Ddgit 0-9825133-7-2.

25. M. K. Haras, *Call to Tawheed*, (In Arabic), Ibn Taymiyyah Publishers, Cairo, Egypt, 1987.

26. Shaikh A. B. M. Al-Mu'taz, *Anchor Prophet Muhammad*, (In Arabic), Darussalam Publishers, Saudi Arabia.

27. Shaikh A. B. M. Al-Mu'taz, ***Anchor Prophet Nooh***, (In Arabic), Darussalam Publishers, Saudi Arabia.

28. Amr Khalid, Stories of the Prophets, (In Arabic), Dar Al-Marefah Publishers, Lebanon, 2009.

29. Abil-Fidaa', ***Stories of the Prophets***, (In Arabic), Original written in the 15th century, AD, but published by Al-Safa Publishers, Egypt 2005.

30. Tarif Khalidi, ***The Muslim Jesus***, Harvard University Press, 2003

31. Fatwa Collections (In Arabic), "Majmoo Al-Fataawa"- vol. 1-35

32. The Beginning and the End (In Arabic), "Al Bidaya wa Annihaya" vol 1-14

33. The Tafsirs (Interpretations of the Qur'an) by Al Tabari, (In Arabic) "Al-Jameeh Li-ahkaam Al-Qur'an Tabari" vol 1-20

34. Sahih Al Bukhari vol 1-9. (In Arabic)

35. Ahkam fi usul al-ahkam Inb Hazam, (In Arabic)

36. Al Itqan fi Ulum al-Qur'an Al-Suytee, (In Arabic)

37. Sahih Muslim, (In Arabic)

38. A'sira al-Halabiya, (In Arabic)

Glossary of Islamic Terms

Term	Explanation
Allah	The Arabic pre-Islamic word for "God." Although the Arabic Bible and the Qur'an both use "Allah," the Biblical and Islamic understandings of such, are fundamentally different.
Caliph or Khalifa	Successors of Muhammad as the political and religious head of the Islamic Ummah. Historically, the Caliph is the designation for the head of state of the Islamic Empire. The last Caliph was Sultan Abdel-Hamid of the Ottoman Empire, who was deposed in 1922 by Kemal Ataturk of Turkey.
Deen	Means "Religion." The Islamic "Deen" is all encompassing, i.e. it is a total system of life and beyond: political, social, economic, educational, military, legislative, judiciary, "cloaked and garbed" in religious terminology.
Fatwa	A religious edict that can be issued by the Ulama' (or a single Aalim) but requiring approvals through a chain of commands in many cases. Most fatwas today are given in Shariah courts to adjudicate disputes, but some are issued to establish rulings on general questions, or to require a Muslim community (Ummah) to implement various actions.
Hajj	5th pillar of Islam. Pilgrimage rite carried out during the Zhul-Hijjah (12th lunar month) to be performed at Mecca, Saudi Arabia. Hajj is required of every able-bodied Muslim, once in a lifetime, if he/she can afford it.
Halal	Permitted, lawful or allowed. In other words, it is a full legal system established by Islam to regulate the life of an individual as well as society. In many instances it might conflict with the laws of host countries. [Dietary laws, polygamy, etc.]

Term	Explanation
Haram	The opposite of "Halal", i.e. Forbidden or un-lawful. [dietary restrictions, Muslim women not allowed to marry non-Muslim men, etc.]
Hijra	Literally, "immigration" or "migration". Historically, it refers to the flight of Muhammad and his followers from Mecca, to Yathrib which was renamed Medina in 622 AD. Muslim scholars and historians consider the Hijra to have been the most important event in Islam's history. Significance of Hijra is both, religious doctrine and political application. The date of the Hijra marked the start of the Islamic lunar calendar, called the Hijri Calendar.
Islam	The "religion" itself. According to the Qur'an, "Islam is the religion of Allah ..." (Surah 3:19). Linguistically, Islam means "submission." It is a word reserved for Allah's only religion and cannot be used for any other purpose, e.g. to declare simply "submission" to Allah.
Jihad	Believed to be divinely sanctioned violence against non-Muslims who are singled out as enemies of Islam.
Jinn or Jinns	According to Islam Allah created the Jinns as invisible creatures from smokeless fire. They have the ability to manifest themselves bodily. The marry, propagate, age and die. They travel at supersonic speed. They are savable. "Believing" Jinn are Muslims. Muhammad claimed that he was sent to both Jinn and mankind.
Kaaba	The most sacred shrine of Islam in Mecca. Direction of the Islamic ritual prayer. Focus of the Hajj. According to the Islam, the Kaaba was built by Adam, rebuilt after the flood by Nooh, and rebuilt again by Ibrahim and Ismaeel.
Kafir (Noun—Kufr)	Unbeliever. Islamically speaking, all non-Muslims are declared as Kafirs.
Mecca	City in Arabia (now Saudi Arabia) and the birthplace of Muhammad.

Term	Explanation
Muhammad	Born around 570 AD and died in 632 AD. Over a period of 23 years (610-632) he developed the Islamic Deen, worked with a group of followers who believed he was the "Seal of the Prophets" to either convince or force the pagan Arabs of Arabia to become Muslims.
Muslim	Person, man or woman who declare the Islamic creed, the Shahadah. Doctrinally, every human being is a Muslim as per Allah's requirement (Fitrah Doctrine: The natural man is Muslim).
Mu'min	Believer in all the beliefs and tenets of Islam.
People of the Book	Term used to identify Jews and Christians.
Prophets and Messengers	They are individuals who were recipients of Wahy to proclaim Islam to their people.
Qibla	Direction of Muslim prayer (Salat) which is toward Mecca.
Qur'an	Allegedly a record of Muhammad's recitations, gathered and standardized after his death.
Quraysh	Name of a Meccean tribe that was responsible for administering the religious rites of the Hajj before Islam. It is also Muhammad's tribe.
Salat	Islamic ritual prayer required to be carried out at five regulated times every day. Second pillar of Islam.
Saum	Islamic ritual fasting during the month of Ramadan (9th month of the Islamic lunar calendar). Fourth pillar of Islam.
Shahadah	The Islamic Creed, "There is no god but Allah and Muhammad is his messenger." Reciting this in the presence of two Muslims would render one as a Muslim. First pillar of Islam.

Term	Explanation
Shariah	It is the codification of Qur'anic and Sunnah/Hadith into various categories covering all the aspects of life, of Muslims and non-Muslims.
Shiites	Second largest sect of Islam (mainly as majority in Iran and Iraq) with sizable minorities in the rest of the Muslim world. Shiites require that the Khalifa should be a blood relative of Muhammad. However, the succession line was broken in the first several decades of Islamic rule.
Shirk	Any attribution of "partners" with Allah is Shirk. It is the most heinous and unforgivable sin in Islam.
Sira	Biography of Muhammad as reported by various Islamic scholars. The earliest available Sira was written by Ibn Hisham and is dated around 100-150 years after the death of Muhammad. This Sira is allegedly based on an earlier Sira by Ibn Ishaq.
Sunnah/ Hadith	The Sunnah is the "Example" of Muhammad, whatever he declared, did, or consented to during his lifetime. The Hadith is the later (many years, after his death) compilation of Sunnah events via chains of narrators. There are many versions of the Hadith with different levels of verification. The Sunnah/Hadith constitute the second source of Shariah legislation.
Sunni's	The majority sect of Islam (around 80%-85%) of all Muslims. Sunni's have adhered to the system of succession not based on being blood relatives of Muhammad.
Taqiyyah	Divinely sanctioned deception.
Tawheed	Term used for the Islamic doctrine of monotheism. This term was introduced by the Ulama' (Scholars) after Muhammad, as it does not exist as such in the Qur'an. Tawheed doctrine is the Islamic alternative to the Trinitarian doctrine of Biblical Christianity.

Term	Explanation
Ulama' (plural of the noun Aalim)	Islamic Scholars who are certified to interpret the Qur'an, Sunnah and the various Jurisprudence schools. These interpretations can be general or academic in nature and also specific in response to legal disputes or in legislating new laws.
Ummah	The Islamic community united by the common Islamic doctrine and goals.
Wahy	Islamic "inspiration" whereby Allah's directives are communicated to the various messengers through angelic beings. The Wahy to Muhammad was the most comprehensive among all the messengers, according to the Qur'an and the Sunnah.
Yathrib/ **Medina**	City some 250 miles north of Mecca. Originally a Jewish city called Yathrib, but later became a combined Jewish and pagan city. When Muhammad immigrated to Yathrib he changed its name to Madinat Annabi (City of the Prophet) or simply, Medina. At that point it became mainly a Jewish/Muslim city.
Zakat	Islamic religious tax for charity and other activities, like Jihad. The nominal Zakat is 2.5% of annual income. Third pillar of Islam.

CPSIA information can be obtained
at www.ICGtesting.com
Printed in the USA
FFOW01n0053010316
21802FF